A WAR AGAINST

ISABEL WOLLASTON

A WAR AGAINST MEMORY?

The Future of Holocaust Remembrance

First published in Great Britain 1996
Society for Promoting Christian Knowledge
Holy Trinity Church
Marylebone Road
London NW1 4DU

British Library Cataloguing-in-Publication Data
A catalogue record of this book is available from
the British Library

ISBN 0-281-04937-8

Typeset by Wilmaset Ltd, Birkenhead, Wirral
Printed in Great Britain by
The Cromwell Press, Melksham, Wiltshire

For Robert

CONTENTS

ACKNOWLEDGEMENTS

The initial research for this book was undertaken during a year spent as a British Academy post-doctoral research fellow at the Oxford Centre for Hebrew and Jewish Studies. I am grateful to both institutions for their support and encouragement, and in particular I owe thanks to Michael Evans of the British Academy, and David Patterson and Jonathan Webber of the Oxford Centre.

My thinking about this subject has benefited greatly from presenting my ideas in a series of papers. I am grateful to the following for providing me with this opportunity: the Holocaust Seminar, Oxford Centre for Hebrew and Jewish Studies; the Lightfoot Society, University of Durham; the Parkes Seminar, University of Southampton; Birmingham Council of Christians and Jews; the Postgraduate Staff Research Seminar, Department of Theology and Religious Studies, University of Bristol; and Open End, Birmingham. I am grateful to all those present for their comments.

In addition, I would like to express my gratitude to friends and colleagues for their support and advice while I was working on this book; in particular, Linda Cooper, Jon Davies, Gavin D'Costa, Konstanty Gebert, Gareth Jones, Paul Joyce, Tony Kushner, Ann Loades, Louise London, Roisin Madigan, Sonia Misak, Jeremy Schonfield, Martin Stringer, Teresa Świebocka, Jonathan Webber, Bill Williams and Connie Wilsack.

Finally, I would like to thank Judith Longman for encouraging me to write this book in the first place, and Philip Law at SPCK for seeing it through to publication.

INTRODUCTION

That we must continue to come to terms with the Holocaust is obvious. The question is: what form will these commemorations take? And addressed to whom? And who will be entitled to speak? And what is the permissible range of discourse?[1]

The 1980s and 1990s have been marked by a series of fiftieth anniversaries relating to Nazism, World War II, and the Holocaust. For example, 1985: the Nuremberg Laws; 1988: the *Anschluss*, Munich, *Kristallnacht*; 1989: the outbreak of World War II; 1990: the Battle of Britain; 1991: the invasion of the Soviet Union, Pearl Harbour; 1992: the Wannsee Conference, El Alamein; 1993: the Warsaw Ghetto Uprising; 1994: D-Day, the Warsaw Rising; 1995: the liberation of Auschwitz, Dresden, VE-Day, Hiroshima and Nagasaki, the end of World War II. Such anniversaries are observed with varying degrees of solemnity and public interest. Few of them are immune to controversy. In Britain, for instance, heated debates have surrounded the unveiling of a statue to Bomber Harris, the initial plans for commemorating D-Day, and the 'twinning' of Coventry and Dresden in ceremonies remembering the effects of saturation bombing.[2]

The diverse reactions to the ceremonies commemorating the fiftieth anniversary of the liberation of Auschwitz serve in many ways to illustrate the 'memory-ignited rage' that simmers close beneath the surface of any attempt to remember these events.[3] Such 'rage' is all too often triggered by anniversaries, as these serve to highlight the extent to which various individuals and groups have different, and often conflicting, memories of the same events. Auschwitz, for many the ultimate symbol of the Holocaust, also serves as the ultimate symbol of the conflict generated by remembrance of these events. Hence the conclusion reached by Neal Ascherson:

> The truth about Auschwitz is that there can never be consensus about the use of its ruins. It has too many symbolisms for too many different, and sometimes mutually suspicious, groups of people . . . But this inner discord, which can never fully be overcome, is what Auschwitz and its memory is all about.[4]

Inevitably, the memory of events is multi-layered, and often fractured. How they are remembered is influenced by the age, gender, nationality

1

and political or religious affiliations of the individual or group remembering. Memory is further coloured by the circumstances of those remembering, both in the past (for example, whether they experienced occupation, served in the armed forces, were a member of the resistance, or an inmate in a concentration camp or death camp) and in the present. Such differences in perspective are reflected, in part, by the choice of terms such as 'the Second World War', 'the Great Patriotic War', '*Hitlerzeit*', and 'the Holocaust'.

The focus of discussion in this book is on the contested nature of what it means to remember the Holocaust. While there is consensus concerning the need to remember the Holocaust, there is widespread, often vehement disagreement over what should be remembered, by whom, and for what purpose. Particularly controversial is the question of what forms of remembrance are appropriate, and what significance should be attached to the Holocaust in relation to other aspects of Jewish culture, history, and belief. Current disagreement over something as seemingly basic as an appropriate name serves as a fitting symbol of the complexity of contemporary perceptions of these events.

The term 'Holocaust' is employed in this book precisely because, given the ambivalence over its use, it best illustrates the complexity inherent in remembering these events. It is an obvious, although often overlooked, truism that the Holocaust is not one event, but rather 'a generalization that unites a variety of discrete events under one rubric'.[5] As such, 'Holocaust', and terms like it, tend to dissolve many distinct events and experiences into one. The very act of naming thus inevitably entails a degree of simplification. For this reason, it is often suggested that no one word or label is sufficient to describe these events. However, recurrent debates over appropriate nomenclature would seem to imply that some names are more appropriate than others. In the words of Dominic LaCapra, we are entering 'an area where there are no easy, uninvolved, or purely objective choices'.[6] Yet such choices have to be made, for the range of possibilities is seemingly endless: 'Holocaust', 'holocaust', '*Shoah*', '*Hurban*', 'the Tremendum', 'the Event', 'the Kingdom of Night', '*l'univers concentrationnaire*', 'the Lager', '*Kz-zeit*', 'genocide', 'the destruction of the European Jews', 'extermination', 'the Final Solution' . . . are but a few examples.

As James Young notes, 'The names we assign this period automatically figure and contextualize events, locating them within the continua of particular historical, literary and interpretive traditions.'[7] As suggested above, it is for precisely this reason that some remain adamant that we should resist the temptation to impose any name upon these events. If to name is to place certain experiences within a particular narrative or interpretive framework, then it can also serve to domesticate or conventionalize the inexpressible. According to Amos Oz, 'all these words attempt to bypass, to soften, to prettify, or to place everything into one known familiar historic pattern.'[8] Yet, even if Oz is correct, to be remembered events have to be thought about and spoken about. To name is to remember, however partially or provisionally. Each of the above names 'remembers' in a way that signifies the adoption (consciously or unconsciously) of a particular discourse, with attendant implications that may be ethical, historical, philosophical, political, rhetorical, or theological.

By way of example, to speak of *'Hurban'* or *'l'univers concentrationnaire'* is to adopt the discourse of the victims, whereas to speak of 'extermination' or 'the Final Solution' is to adopt the language of Nazi bureaucracy. To speak of *'Hurban'* is to contextualize events within the continuum of Jewish history and belief, whereas *'Shoah'* and 'Holocaust' were both coined, in part, to suggest a rupture within that continuum. To capitalize 'Holocaust' is to assert the uniqueness of these events; to refuse to do so is to distance oneself from such an assertion. The situation is complicated further by the changing, often multiple meanings of particular terms. Today, the adoption of *'Shoah'* generally signifies the rejection of any attribution of religious meanings to these events, although a number of biblical usages of the term carry associations of a disaster sent by God.[9]

'Holocaust', arguably more than any other, is both a term that can be understood in a variety of ways, and one that is frequently accused of misrepresenting the reality it purports to express. On the one hand it is a term that belongs to the discourse of victims; on the other it is the term 'currently most widely employed'.[10] Etymologically, 'Holocaust' is problematic for many because of its sacrificial overtones, suggestive of a 'burnt offering'. Yet, for others, the significance of the term lies in its awe-ful connotations and its associations with fire. However, as Elie Wiesel, one of the term's earliest advocates, points out, such associations are often lost in the transition from survivor discourse to popular culture.[11] The prevalent popular usage of the term serves to routinize its meaning; a process which in itself often counteracts any sacrificial connotations. Finally, 'Holocaust' tends to be the term favoured by those engaged, consciously or unconsciously, in the mythologization of these events (an issue that will be discussed at greater length in Chapter 6).

This brief survey of the 'verbal iconography of the Holocaust' serves to indicate the range of possible interpretations of these events.[12] The aim of the following discussion is to explore further what is meant by the seemingly unambiguous – yet far from straightforward – assertion that we should remember the Holocaust.

NOTES

1. P. Lopate, 'Resistance to the Holocaust' (*Tikkun* 1989, 4:3), pp. 55–65, p. 58.

2. For a more detailed discussion of such controversies, see: P. Clough, 'Now Dresden's Horror is Recalled' (*Sunday Times* 29.1.95); J. Ezard, 'The Firestorm Rages On' (*Guardian* 18.5.92); R. Harris, 'The Big Difference between "Butcher" Harris and a Nazi' (*Sunday Times* 31.5.92); I. Katz, 'A Good Night's Work' (*Guardian* 26.7.94); R. Littlejohn, 'Don't Ask Me to Say Sorry for the Dresden Bombing' (*Daily Mail* 10.2.95); J. Taylor, 'Monuments to Massacre' (*New Statesman and Society* 22.5.92), pp. 31–2.

3. J. E. Young, 'The Future of Auschwitz' (*Tikkun* 1992, 7:6), pp. 31–3, p. 77. For more detail on the controversy generated by the commemoration of the fiftieth anniversary of Auschwitz, see: I. Buruma, 'The Misleading Mystique of Mass Extermination' (*Spectator* 28.1.95), pp. 9–11; J. Jackson, 'Return to Auschwitz' (*Time* 6.2.95), pp. 18–19; A. Nagorski, 'A Tortured Legacy' (*Newsweek* 16.1.95), pp. 24–5; *The Tablet* 4.2.95, p. 157.

4. N. Ascherson, 'Remains of the Abomination' (*Independent on Sunday Review* 22.1.95), pp. 12–16, pp. 15–16.

5. G. Kren, 'The Holocaust as History' in A. Rosenberg and G. Myers (eds.), *Echoes from the Holocaust* (Philadelphia: Temple University Press, 1988), pp. 3–50, p. 4.

6. D. LaCapra, 'Representing the Holocaust' in S. Friedlander (ed.), *Probing the Limits of Representation* (Cambridge: Harvard University Press, 1992), note 4, p. 357.

7. J. E. Young, *Writing and Rewriting the Holocaust* (Bloomington: Indiana University Press, 1988), p. 85.

8. A. Oz, *The Slopes of Lebanon* (Vintage, 1991), p. 159. See also: Lopate, 'Resistance to the Holocaust', p. 55; J. Neusner, *The Jewish War Against the Jews* (New York: KTAV, 1994), pp. 51–2; and E. Wiesel, in P. de Saint-Cheron and E. Wiesel, *Evil and Exile* (Notre Dame: University of Notre Dame Press, 1990), p. 38.

9. U. Tal, 'On the Study of Holocaust and Genocide: Excursus on Hermeneutical Aspects of the Term *Sho'ah*' (*Yad Vashem Studies* 1979, 13), pp. 7–52, pp. 46–52.

10. E. Fackenheim, 'Holocaust' in A. Cohen and P. Mendes-Flohr (eds.), *Contemporary Jewish Religious Thought* (New York: Free Press, 1988), pp. 399–408, p. 399.
11. Etymologically, 'Holocaust' derives from the Greek translation of *ola* (Gen. 22.1; 1 Sam. 7.9). For Wiesel, the term had a number of advantages: (a) it alluded to the *Akedah*, the Binding of Isaac; (b) it emphasized 'the mystical, religious texture of the tragedy'; (c) 'this catastrophe was redolent of fire above all else . . . What does "Holocaust" mean? Total offering by fire'; (d) 'the term also implies total catastrophe'. (de Saint-Cheron and Wiesel, *Evil and Exile*, p. 39). Today, Wiesel argues that 'Holocaust' has been misused, even corrupted: 'It has been so trivialized and commercialized. These days it's used to refer to just about anything.' As a result, he now prefers the term 'Hurban' (see *Evil and Exile*, pp. 39 and 88).

For a critique of 'Holocaust', see Z. Garber and B. Zuckerman, 'Why Do We Call the Holocaust "the Holocaust"?' (*Modern Judaism* May 1989), pp. 197–211.
12. J. E. Young, 'The Art of Memory' in Young (ed.), *The Art of Memory* (Munich and New York: Prestel-Verlag, 1994), pp. 19–37, p. 21.

1

WHY REMEMBER?

Few, apart from revisionist histor-
ians, would challenge the need to remember the Holocaust. On the
surface, the slogan 'Zakhor!' ('Remember!') needs little, if any,
explanation. Yet, while the commitment to remember the Holocaust is
nearly universal, the motivations for remembering vary. One thread
that does remain constant is the insistence that the dead must not be
forgotten:[1] for, in the words of the survivor, Elie Wiesel, to forget the
dead is 'to have them die a second time'.[2] Yet any answer to the
question 'why remember?' is inevitably influenced by perspective, by
factors such as whether the speaker is a survivor or a non-survivor (i.e.
someone who was not 'there'), Jewish or non-Jewish. For example,
while there is common ground between the commitment of a Jew and a
Christian to remember, there will also be significant differences in the
content of what is remembered and the forms in which remembrance is
expressed.

The recent controversy over the presence of Carmelite nuns at
Auschwitz serves to highlight the conflicts generated by such differences.[3] For the nuns and their supporters, nothing could be more
appropriate than the establishment of a Carmel on this site. They were,
after all, acting on precisely the same impulse that led to the establishment of a Carmel on the site of the public gallows at Tyburn. By
engaging in prayer and penance, the nuns believed that they were
honouring the souls of all those who died, but particularly the
memories of the Catholic victims of Auschwitz, who included
Maksymilian Kolbe (canonized in 1982), and Edith Stein (beatified in
1987). However, for many Jews, the establishment of a Christian place
of worship on the site was at best insensitive and, at worst, offensive.
Critics of the Carmel were quick to contrast such an institutional act of
remembrance with the silence of the majority of Churches and their
leaders during the Holocaust. Some saw the establishment of the
Carmel as an attempt to 'Christianize' Auschwitz, to present Christians
as 'co-victims' with Jews and thus deflect accusations of inaction or
culpability. Thus what was originally intended as an act of conciliation
had the diametrically opposite effect of polarization, despite the
presence of a common commitment to remembrance.

The debate provoked by the Carmel at Auschwitz is only one

example of a recent controversy over what constitutes appropriate remembrance of the Holocaust. Such controversies highlight the need to be clear as to our motivation: the debate over the Carmel was marked by a lack of understanding, even awareness, of the variety of motivations and possible expressions of remembrance. The purpose of this chapter is, therefore, to consider in some detail the various motivations that currently dominate remembrance of the Holocaust.

—— *Remembering for the Future?* ——

'Never again': this oft-quoted slogan encapsulates the rhetoric of remembrance, a rhetoric that purports to believe that remembrance is the key to preventing repetition. Many survivors, educators, historians and politicians assert that the best insurance against any possible repetition lies in a combination of constant vigilance and a commitment to keeping the memory of the Holocaust at the forefront of our consciousness. Such a perspective is summed up by Primo Levi: 'It happened therefore it can happen again: this is the core of what we have to say.'[4] This emphasis on 'never again' is a constant thread running throughout remembrance of the Holocaust. The observation of a reporter at the commemorations of the fiftieth anniversary of the liberation of Auschwitz could apply equally well to any number of similar occasions: 'The talk was all of remembrance, of the importance of not forgetting, of the role that Auschwitz has as a warning to future generations.'[5] Yet, while affirming the importance of remembrance, a number of survivors and commentators warn against the danger or illusory quality of the rhetoric of 'never again'. To what extent does the rhetoric of remembrance serve to disguise a marked reluctance on the part of governments to intervene, or become involved, in post-Holocaust examples of genocide (the most recent being Bosnia and Rwanda)? Less optimistic observers concur with the observation of one survivor that, rather than 'never again', 'the lesson of Auschwitz is that you can get away with it'.[6]

The rhetoric of 'never again' reflects a widespread assumption that keeping the memory of these events alive, and studying their causes and effects, is the best way to sensitize society to the early warning signs of anything remotely similar to the rise of Nazism or the Holocaust. Such an assumption underlies the work of many Holocaust-related institutions: memorials, museums, or educational bodies such as the British-based Holocaust Educational Trust, the Dutch-based Anne Frank Educational Trust, or the American-based Facing History and Ourselves National Foundation. The Auschwitz State Museum believes that it

7

stands as 'an eternal warning against the rebirth of Nazism'. The guidebook to the Permanent Exhibition of the United States Holocaust Memorial Museum (USHMM) in Washington DC states that its aim is 'to memorialize the past by educating a new generation partly in the hope of transforming the future by sensitizing those who will shape it'.[7] Steven Spielberg explains his motivation for making the film *Schindler's List* in similar terms: 'This is the first movie with a message I've ever attempted. It is a very simple message – that something like this should never happen again.'[8] In another interview, he elaborates on this point further: 'I wanted to make my children aware that they could make a difference.'[9] Given that such assumptions are so widespread, and couched in such emotive language, it becomes all the more important to understand the thinking behind them.

It seems apparent that 'never again' is a deceptively simple assertion masking a range of assumptions and intentions. One such assumption concerns the need for *active* remembrance: it is necessary to make a conscious effort to know what happened, and then communicate that knowledge to others. Thus, for Spielberg, it was not sufficient to make *Schindler's List*. He also felt compelled to travel the world drawing attention to the central message of the film. Spielberg used the media platform of his Oscar-winning speech to issue a heartfelt appeal to society as a whole to remember. A couple of years earlier, the British Chief Rabbi, Jonathan Sacks, called for a similar commitment to active remembrance in his response to the growing crisis in the former Yugoslavia: 'Our moral credibility after the Holocaust rests on a collective commitment never again to be passive witnesses to mass extermination, concentration camps, and "ethnic cleansing".'[10] While Sacks and others were quick to insist that no direct comparison could be drawn between the Holocaust and 'ethnic cleansing', they were equally adamant that the memory of the former necessitated active campaigning against the latter. Sacks, Spielberg and the USHMM all argue that the remembrance of the Holocaust should serve to sensitize individuals and society to injustice in any form. For Sacks, such sensitivity takes the form of a collective, active commitment to oppose actions such as 'ethnic cleansing'. For Spielberg, it takes the form of personal moral responsibility. For the USHMM, it takes the form of a vigilant defence of 'the core American – indeed the core human – values of individual dignity, social justice, and civil rights'.[11]

A related assumption underlying 'never again' is the hope that education sensitizes people. Museums such as the USHMM and individuals such as Spielberg assume that it is primarily through education that the process of sensitization will take place. This belief is encapsulated in the choice of inscription at the entrance to the permanent exhibition at the Auschwitz State Museum: 'The one who does not remember history is bound to live through it again' (George Santayana). For many, Holocaust education is the most effective *active* form of remembrance. Such education can take a variety of forms, from the formally academic (research, publishing, teaching, conferences) to the more popular (films such as *Schindler's List*, trips to sites connected with the Holocaust, museums and exhibitions). In such educational activities, the testimony of victims and survivors plays a central role (whether delivered in person, on audio or video tape, or read as literature). In emphasizing the educational lessons to be learned, the Holocaust is presented as an example – of antisemitism, racism, or radical evil. The Holocaust is understood as 'the paradigm for contemporary tragic history'.[12] In the words of an editorial in *Dimensions*, 'The main aim of Holocaust education today is the warning it provides about the destructive consequences of prejudice and discrimination.'[13]

We must ask, however, whether such bold claims are anything more than empty rhetoric. *What* is never to happen again, and to *whom* should it never happen? Marc Ellis suggests that, from a Jewish perspective, 'never again' is shorthand for 'never again *for us*'. He warns that such a slogan can serve to desensitize Jews to the suffering of others, notably the Palestinians.[14] Is there a danger that discourse about the Holocaust will degenerate into a competition over who has 'a more exclusive property right to suffering'?[15] Indeed, is this precisely what recent controversies about remembrance of the Holocaust have primarily been about? One point at issue here is clearly the relationship between the unique and the universal. A commitment to remembering the Holocaust requires a decision as to who and what we are talking about. For Elie Wiesel, it is only by speaking of the unique aspects of the Holocaust that it becomes possible to address its universal implications. Yet at the same time, he concedes 'the right of a Cambodian to say about Cambodia what I have said about Auschwitz'.[16] For Primo Levi, the key issue is the potentially universal ramifications of a particular experience: what happened may not only happen again, but 'it can happen anywhere'.[17]

The pressing issue for survivors and educators alike is whether speaking and learning about what happened will succeed in making it less likely that such events happen again. Is there any evidence to support the claim that we do, in fact, learn from history, or that remembering will ensure against repetition? Much of the media comment on the fiftieth anniversary of the liberation of Auschwitz suggested otherwise. Typical examples were Robert Block: ' "Never

9

Again'' Obviously Doesn't Apply in Rwanda', and William Pfaff: 'Bosnia, Groszny, Beit Lid: And They Say It'll Never Happen Again?'[18] These articles both argue that, given current examples of 'ethnic cleansing', the international community's commitment to remembering the Holocaust is little more than empty rhetoric, mourning past atrocities while ignoring those taking place in the present.

Wiesel, one of the most prominent exponents of the rhetoric of remembrance, is acutely aware of this danger. Hence he frequently takes advantage of the opportunities presented by a public forum, such as the state commemoration of the fiftieth anniversary of the liberation of Auschwitz, to insist that a rhetoric of remembrance that is not matched by a practical commitment to human rights is empty, an insult even.[19] For Michael Berenbaum, the question of whether the slogan 'never again' is merely rhetoric, or serves as a stimulus to action, is a challenge to be answered by each individual as they encounter the Holocaust. For him, the purpose of remembrance is to articulate and pose the question. He concludes his guide to the USHMM with a quotation from an inmate of Sachsenhausen:

> I have told you this story not to weaken you.
> But to strengthen you.
> Now it is up to you![20]

Others are even less optimistic than this. Should we not be wary of placing such emphasis upon the purpose or function of remembrance? Is there not a seductive quality to any rhetoric of remembrance that seeks to sanctify the victims and demonize the perpetrators? Certain forms of the rhetoric of remembrance simplify the Holocaust by presenting it in dualistic terms as a battle of absolute good and absolute evil, highlighting the 'lessons' to be learned by reference to the faith and heroism of victims *in extremis*. Such an approach reduces and simplifies what was, in fact, 'an extraordinarily distorted and ugly reality'.[21] By focusing on the humanitarian and heroic aspects of the Holocaust (as, for example, in *Schindler's List*), there is a danger of mistaking the exceptional for the norm. To counter any such tendency the literary critic, Lawrence Langer, repeatedly insists that 'remembering the Holocaust is the most unredemptive task one can possibly imagine'.[22] For Langer, to remember the Holocaust is to remember that which has been irretrievably lost. He contrasts the 'rhetoric of heroic behaviour' (typified by the glorification of the Warsaw Ghetto Fighters) with the 'ruins of memory' (the sub-text of loss that permeates much Holocaust testimony). However, if we are to remember the Holocaust in all its complexity, then surely both the 'rhetoric of heroic behaviour' and the 'ruins of memory' have a place. A one-sided emphasis upon the 'rhetoric of heroic behaviour' may lead to the naive assumption that remembrance will be redemptive in terms of the future, if not the past: it will ensure against any potential repetition. In view of Langer's emphasis upon the 'ruins of memory', it is hardly surprising to hear a survivor conclude that 'the lesson of Auschwitz is that you can get away with it'. Yet, at the same time, the 'rhetoric of heroic behaviour' has a place, both in the writings of victims and survivors, and in the more general rhetoric of remembrance. Both the 'rhetoric of heroic behaviour' and the 'ruins of memory' have their foundations in the responses of those who experienced the Holocaust. The aim is to avoid privileging one at the expense of the other.[23]

—— Remembering as a Sacred Duty ——

For the philosopher Emil Fackenheim, remembering the Holocaust is more than an educational necessity, it is a sacred duty: 'We are commanded . . . to remember in our very guts and bones the martyrs of the Holocaust, lest their memory perish.'[24] Such a claim must be set in context: the injunction to remember plays a central role in the Jewish tradition and is enshrined in a series of individual and collective obligations.[25]

The individual is called upon to observe a variety of acts of remembrance, such as saying kaddish, lighting *yahrzeit* candles, and visiting the graves of the deceased. The community's obligation to remember is twofold, extending both to God's acts of redemption and to historical catastrophe, and is given classic expression in the liturgical calendar. Rabbi Irving Greenberg suggests that the calendar serves to shape and deepen group memory: 'In an annual cycle, every Jew lives through all of Jewish history and makes it his or her own personal experience.'[26] The centrality of memory is enshrined in the remembrance of the key events in Jewish history, both positive and negative. Thus, the festival of Passover fulfils the command to remember God's saving action in freeing his people from slavery in Egypt (Exod. 13.3). Conversely, four fast days (3 Tishri, 10 Tevet, 17 Tammuz, 9 Av) are set aside for the remembrance of events surrounding the destruction of the Jerusalem Temple in 586 BCE. Remembrance of subsequent catastrophes is absorbed into this liturgical provision for commemorating the destruction of the Temple. *Kinot* (dirges) dedicated to the victims of the Crusader and Chmielnicki massacres were incorporated into the liturgy of 9 Av. From a traditional perspective, remembrance of the Holocaust is to be absorbed into the liturgy in a similar way. In 1948 the Israeli

11

Chief Rabbinate designed 10 Tevet 'Yom Kaddish Klali' (a day of communal kaddish) for the remembrance of victims of the Holocaust with no surviving relatives or whose date of death was unknown.

The centrality of memory is further emphasized by the annual reading of the Torah in synagogue, beginning and ending on Simhat Torah. Reading the Torah in this way serves to reinforce the centrality of memory, as the text contains numerous injunctions to remember, alongside warnings against forgetfulness. A typical injunction to remember is that found in the *Shema* (Deut. 6.4–11; 11.13–21; Num. 15.37–41):

> Hear, O Israel: The Lord is our God, the Lord alone. You shall love the Lord your God with all your heart, and with all your soul, and with all your might. Keep these words that I am commanding to you today in your heart. Recite them to your children and talk about them when you sit in your house, when you are away, when you lie down and when you rise. Bind them as a sign on your hand, fix them as an emblem on your forehead, and write them on the doorposts of your house and on your gates (Deut. 6.4–9).

The *Shema's* injunction to remember finds an ironic reflection in the poetry of the (non-religious) survivor Primo Levi. In his poem 'Shema' (dated 10 January 1946), Levi calls upon his readers to commit to memory the experiences of the victims of Nazi concentration camps. In doing so he adopts the language of the biblical *Shema*:

> Consider that this has been:
> I commend these words to you.
> Engrave them on your hearts
> When you are in your house, when you walk on your way,
> When you go to bed, when you rise.
> Repeat them to your children.
> Or may your houses crumble,
> Disease render you powerless,
> Your offspring avert their faces from you.[27]

The final curse in Levi's poem is drenched with scriptural allusions. The severest of the biblical curses is arguably the threat that one's name will be blotted out. The paradigmatic curse of this type is that upon Amalek: 'I will utterly blot out the remembrance of Amalek from under heaven: do not forget' (Exod. 17.14). It is not enough that Amalek's name is to be blotted out; the fact that it has been blotted out must be remembered for all time. The rabbis complied with this biblical injunction by incorporating the remembrance of Amalek into the liturgical calendar.

12

The *maftir* (additional reading) for the Sabbath before Purim ('Shabbat Zakhor' or Sabbath of Remembrance) is Deut. 25.17–19:

> Remember what Amalek did to you on your journey out of Egypt, how he attacked you on the way, when you were fast and weary, and struck down all who lagged behind you; he did not fear God. Therefore when the Lord your God has given you rest from all your enemies on every hand, in the land that the Lord your God is giving you as an inheritance to possess, you shall blot out the remembrance of Amalek from under heaven: do not forget.

Precisely because of this sense that to have one's name blotted out is the worst of fates, there was, and is, 'a holy, compulsive drive to record and testify' to the Holocaust.[28] The Holocaust can be understood as a struggle to determine who would fulfil the role of Amalek: whereas the Nazis were determined that the fate of the Jews would be remembered only on their terms, the victims were determined, at the very least, to bear witness to the 'scorched vestiges' of their own passing.[29]

—— The Holocaust as a War against —— Memory

The Holocaust can be understood as a struggle over *who* would remember, and *what* would be remembered. For this reason, Primo Levi and Elie Wiesel describe the Holocaust as 'a war against memory'.[30] The Nazis were determined to leave no trace of the destruction of the Jews. If the Jews were to be remembered at all, it would be on the Nazis' own terms, either in the propaganda of *Der Sturmer*, or in the planned Jewish museum in Prague. Jewish memory of these events was to be erased: 'No one would be left to tell the tale.'[31] This is one of the reasons why the majority of the death camps were located in remote, sparsely populated regions. On completion of their task, the killing installations were to be dismantled and the sites ploughed over (as at Treblinka) or planted with trees (as at Sobibor). There was a similar intention with regard to Maidanek and Auschwitz, but the Nazis' plans were thwarted by the speed of the Soviet advance. At Auschwitz, the Nazis only had sufficient time to destroy the gas chambers and crematoria, and to evacuate the majority of the inmates on death-marches westward into the heart of the German Reich.[32] The success of the Nazis in destroying or dismantling the killing installations led Claude Lanzmann to lament that, in making the film *Shoah*, he was confronted by 'the disappearance of traces' and 'with the traces of

13

traces'.[33] As a result, much of his film is dominated by the camera slowly panning over the sites of the death camps as they are today. In the case of many of the sites in the film (such as Chelmno and Sobibor), there is little immediately apparent physical evidence that the events described in the film's narrative actually took place there.

According to Heinrich Himmler, addressing a gathering of SS officers at Posen in October 1943, the destruction of the Jews was to be 'an unwritten and never to be written page of glory in our history'.[34] But by bearing witness to their own destruction, the victims ensured that Jewish memory of these events would survive, that 'a luminous page in the dark history of our times' would be written.[35] In view of the Nazis' determination to leave no trace, testimony can be seen as a form of resistance, 'an act of war against fascism'.[36] It is only because survivors such as Simon Srebnik (one of only two survivors of Chelmno) were prepared to bear witness for Lanzmann that we now have on film a record of events there told from the perspective of the victims.

A large number of testimonies written during the war has survived – even though their authors often did not – from the more famous examples, such as the diary of Anne Frank, to the less well known, such as *Oneg Shabbat* (*O.S.*) (the clandestine archive of the Warsaw Ghetto), or the accounts of the Sonderkommando at Auschwitz. It is, however, also important to note that much of what was written did not survive (for example, the archive of the ZOB, the Jewish Combat Organization in the Warsaw Ghetto, was destroyed during the Warsaw Uprising). Inevitably the thought that their testimony would not survive preoccupied many of those who wrote. This fear is expressed in the final entry of Chaim Kaplan's diary: 'If my life ends – what will become of my diary?'[37] Writing in January 1943, Emmanuel Ringelblum (the founder of *Oneg Shabbat*) commented on how much testimony had been lost: 'A great deal was written, but the largest part was destroyed along with the end of Warsaw Jewry in the Deportation. All that remained was the material preserved in O.S.'[38] While some material apart from *Oneg Shabbat* did survive (such as Kaplan's diary), only two of the three parts of the archive that were buried have been recovered.

The victims' concern that their testimony would be lost or destroyed was often accompanied by fear that the Jewish community itself would not survive. At first, diarists expressed their conviction that 'our existence as a people will not be destroyed. Individuals will be destroyed, but the Jewish community will live on.'[39] However, as news began to travel of mass deportations and of the existence of death camps, such as Belzec and Treblinka, this conviction began to waver. By mid-July 1942, Oskar Singer felt compelled to ask, 'Will there be anyone able to tell the world how we lived and died here?'[40] This fear is alluded to by two of the survivors in *Shoah* (Simon Srebnik and Simha Rottem) when they recall their sense of being 'the last Jew'.[41]

Those who wrote during the Holocaust had a clear sense both of the significance and the limitations of testimony as resistance. They did not write with the benefit of hindsight. The victims did not know that the Nazis would be defeated, although they hoped that this would be the case. Their testimony was intended to serve a dual purpose. First, it was an attempt to inform both the outside world and future generations of their fate. Second, it was 'a desperate struggle at self-immortalization, at leaving some human record to defy the degradation and finality of death that surrounded and awaited the writer'.[42] Kaplan intended his diary to be 'a scroll of agony to remember the past in the future'.[43] Zalmen Gradowski, a member of the Sonderkommando at Auschwitz-Birkenau, hoped by burying his testimony 'to immortalize the dear, beloved names of those, for whom, at this moment, I cannot even expend a tear'. At the same time, he remained conscious that 'it may be that these, the lines that I am now writing, will be the sole witnesses to what was my life'.[44] In his journal entry for 26 June 1942, Ringelblum describes the sense of achievement felt by members of 'Oneg Shabbat' on hearing a radio broadcast based on information they had smuggled out of Poland:

> It is not important whether or not the revelation of the incredible slaughter of Jews will have the desired effect – whether or not the methodical liquidation of entire Jewish communities will stop. One thing we know – we have fulfilled our duty. We have overcome every obstacle to achieve our end. Nor will our deaths be meaningless like the deaths of tens of thousands of Jews. We have struck the enemy a hard blow. We have revealed his Satanic plan to annihilate Polish Jewry, a plan which he meant to complete in silence.[45]

The understanding of testimony as resistance continues into the present and can take a number of forms. Many survivors felt compelled to continue bearing witness, both on their own behalf and in order to fulfil what they saw as an obligation to the dead. For Wiesel there is a choice: with whom do we choose to side, the victims or the perpetrators? We are either actively committed to remembering those who died, or we help to ensure that such events are forgotten, that no trace remains. In addition, bearing witness can be a form of mourning. Annette Wieviorka describes the *yizkher biher* (memory books) compiled by survivors as 'collective memorials, paper monuments, to the

15

destroyed communities'.[46] For Wiesel, writing is 'a *matzeva*, an invisible tombstone erected to the dead unburied'.[47] A further way of mourning and honouring the dead is to build memorials, often – as is the case in Poland – from the fragments of Jewish tombstones destroyed by the Nazis.[48]

Part of the success of the Nazis lies in the fact that we are often forced to remember the dead as an anonymous mass: 'the six million'. Museums such as Auschwitz remember the dead through the artefacts that survived them: the barracks, the ruins of the gas chambers and crematoria, piles of the victims' belongings (suitcases, spectacles, even hair). In addition there are photographs taken by the Nazis and films taken by the Allies on liberating the camps. Relatively little evidence has survived to tell us who the dead were or how they experienced their fate. The museum displays such material as there is, in the form of letters, the testimony of the Sonderkommando, and so on. However, as James Young points out, 'the sum of these dismembered fragments can never approach the whole of what was lost.'[49]

A similar commitment to personalizing the abstract figure of six million and thereby countering 'the anonymity of victimage' is found in the work of many survivor-writers.[50] In his introduction to *Moments of Reprieve*, Levi observes that his aim was to provide 'friends, people I'd travelled with, even adversaries' with the 'ambiguous perennial existence of literary characters'.[51] For Wiesel, writing offers the opportunity 'to rebuild a vanished universe'. In doing so, his goal is 'to bring back, at least for a while, some of the men and women the killers robbed of their life and their names'.[52] In recreating the individuals and the communities that were destroyed, the survivor-writer continues to wage 'a war against memory'. To cite Wiesel again, 'the enemy wanted a society purged of their presence, and I have brought some of them back.'[53]

Herein lies the survivor-writer's dilemma: recreating the past only serves to re-emphasize how much has been lost, the extent to which the Nazis succeeded in their aim of destroying the Jews and in leaving no trace of the process of that destruction. For example, in the case of Eastern Europe, an entire culture was effectively wiped out. Whereas pre-war Poland was arguably the spiritual centre of world Jewry, post-war Poland is often spoken of as a graveyard.[54] The Holocaust resulted in the amputation of what had been one of world Jewry's most vital 'limbs'. The survivors, the writings left behind by the victims and some material remains are the only trace of what was destroyed and the process of that destruction. Lawrence Langer refers to 'the ruins of memory', the consciousness of 'a lost piece of the past that can be evoked but not restored'.[55] As a consequence, the survivor-writer's strategy of recreation can be seen as 'an attempt to put the pages of the book back together'.[56] In recreating the lives of those who died and the values by which they lived, the survivor-writer can pay homage, perhaps even change the way the non-survivor perceives the dead (that is, as individuals rather than as an anonymous, dehumanized mass). However, no amount of skilful literary recreation can succeed in bringing the dead back to life. In many ways, the very attempt highlights the gulf of experience separating past and present: it is the recreated, rather than the remembered past that is sheltered from disaster.

NOTES

1. The insistence that the dead must not be forgotten is also the primary motivation behind many war memorials. The commitment to remembering the war dead is traditionally encapsulated by Lawrence Binyon's poem, 'For the Fallen':

   They shall not grow old, as we that are left grow old.
   Age shall not weary them, nor the years condemn.
   At the going down of the sun and in the morning
   We shall remember them.

   However, as Geoff Dyer points out, these words were written in September 1914, that is, 'before the fallen actually fell'. The poem is therefore 'a work not of remembrance but of anticipation'. (Dyer, *The Missing of the Somme*, Hamish Hamilton, 1994, p. 7). An analogous, but very different, anticipation of remembrance is found in the writings of many of the victims of the Holocaust.

   For a more detailed discussion of war and remembrance, see: D. Boorman, *At the Going Down of the Sun* (Ebor Press, 1988); A. Borg, *War Memorials* (Leo Cooper, 1991); P. Fussell, *The Great War and Modern Memory* (OUP, 1975); S. Hynes, *A War Imagined* (Bodley Head, 1990); C. McIntyre, *Monuments of War* (Hale, 1990); G. Mosse, *Fallen Soldiers* (OUP, 1990).

2. P. de Saint-Cheron and E. Wiesel, *Evil and Exile* (Notre Dame: University of Notre Dame Press, 1990), p. 15.

3. For a more detailed discussion of the Carmelite controversy, see: W. T. Bartoszewski, *The Convent at Auschwitz* (Bowerdean Press, 1990); C. Rittner and J. Roth (eds.), *Memory Offended* (New York: Praeger 1991); I. Wollaston, 'Sharing Sacred Space? The Carmelite Controversy and the

Politics of Commemoration' (*Patterns of Prejudice*, 1994, 28:3–4), pp. 19–27.

4. P. Levi, *The Drowned and the Saved* (Michael Joseph, 1988), p. 167.

5. T. Fishlock, 'Survivors United in Memories and Grief' (*Daily Telegraph* 28.1.95).

6. Quoted in J. Miles, 'Auschwitz and Sarajevo' (*Tikkun* 1994, 9:2), pp. 17–20 and 91–2, p. 17.

7. T. and H. Świebocki (eds.), *Auschwitz: Voices from the Ground* (Oświęcim: Państowe Muzeum Oświęcim-Brzezinka, 1992), p. 104; M. Berenbaum, *The World Must Know: The History of the Holocaust as Told in the United States Holocaust Memorial Museum* (Boston: Little, Brown & Company, 1993), p. 1.

8. Z. Heller, 'The Real Thing' (*Independent on Sunday Review* 23.5.93), pp. 24–8, p. 27.

9. N. Wapshott, 'Return of the Prodigal' (*The Times Magazine* 15.1.94), pp. 7–9, p. 9.

10. *Daily Telegraph* 8.8.92.

11. Berenbaum, *The World Must Know*, p. 235.

12. J. Doneson, *The Holocaust in American Film* (Philadelphia: JPSA, 1987), p. 154.

13. D. Klein, 'The Nineties' (*Dimensions* 1989, 5:1), p. 2.

14. Marc Ellis argues that the Holocaust is becoming increasingly politicized, particularly in Israel. He suggests that the Holocaust is used as 'a way of crushing dissent and mobilizing the community to repress Palestinian aspirations to human dignity and justice'. See: M. Ellis, 'After Auschwitz and the Palestinian Uprising' in D. Cohn-Sherbok (ed.), *Problems in Contemporary Jewish Theology* (Edwin Mellen Press, 1991), pp. 127–57; Ellis, *Ending Auschwitz: The Future of Jewish and Christian Life* (Louisville: Westminster/John Knox Press, 1994); B. Evron, 'The Holocaust: Learning the Wrong Lessons' (*Journal of Palestinian Studies* Spring 1981, 10), pp. 16–26.

15. C. Maier, *The Unmasterable Past* (Cambridge, Massachusetts: Harvard University Press, 1988), p. 164.

16. De Saint-Cheron and Wiesel, *Evil and Exile*, p. 52. For a more detailed discussion of the uniqueness of the Holocaust, see Steven Katz' magisterial *The Holocaust in Historical Context*, Vol. 1 (OUP, 1994), pp. 1–174, 579–81. See also: Z. Bauman, *Modernity and the Holocaust* (Polity Press, 1989), pp. 83–116; M. Berenbaum, *After Tragedy and Triumph* (CUP, 1990), pp. 17–60; E. Fackenheim, *To Mend the World*, Second Edition (New York: Schocken, 1989), pp. xi–xxv, 9–14; D. Lackey, 'Extraordinary Evil or Common Malevolence: Evaluating the Jewish Holocaust' (*Journal of Applied Philosophy 1986, 3:2*), pp. 167–81.

17. Levi, *The Drowned and the Saved*, p. 167.
18. R. Block, ' "Never Again" Obviously Doesn't Apply in Rwanda' (*Independent* 28.1.95); W. Pfaff, 'Bosnia, Grozny, Beit Lid: And They Say It'll Never Happen Again?' (*International Herald Tribune* 28–29.1.95).
19. For the text of Wiesel's speech at Auschwitz, see *Sunday Times* 29.1.95.
20. Berenbaum, *The World Must Know*, pp. 3, 223.
21. M. Lerner, 'Victims and Victimizers' (*Tikkun* 1994, 9:2), pp. 7–9, p. 8.
22. L. Langer, 'Tainted Memory: Remembering the Warsaw Ghetto' (*Tikkun* 1993, 8:3), pp. 37–40, 85–90, p. 40.
23. For a more detailed discussion of the 'privileging' of testimony, see I. Wollaston, 'Religious Language after the Holocaust' in F. Young (ed.), *Dare We Speak of God in Public?* (Mowbray, 1995), pp. 80–9, pp. 84–6.
24. E. Fackenheim, 'Jewish Values in a Post-Holocaust Future' (*Judaism* 1967, 16:3), pp. 266–99, p. 272.
25. For a more detailed discussion of the centrality of memory in the Jewish tradition, see: B. Childs, *Memory and Tradition in Israel* (SCM, 1962); A. Mintz, *Hurban* (New York: Columbia University Press, 1984), pp. 1–105; D. Roskies, *Against the Apocalypse* (Cambridge, Massachusetts: Harvard University Press, 1984), pp. 1–78; Y. Yerushalmi, *Zakhor* (New York: Schocken, 1982). For a discussion of *Zakhor*, see *History and Memory* 1992, 4:2, pp. 129–48.
26. I. Greenberg, *The Jewish Way: Living the Holidays* (New York: Summit Books, 1988), p. 22.
27. P. Levi, *Collected Poems* (Faber & Faber, 1992), p. 9.
28. Rabbi Norman Lamm, in I. Levkov (ed.), *Bitburg and Beyond* (New York: Shapolsky Books, 1987), p. 76.
29. E. Wiesel, *One Generation After* (New York: Schocken Books, 1987), p. 76.
30. Levi, *The Drowned and the Saved*, p. 18; de Saint-Cheron and Wiesel, *Evil and Exile*, p. 155.
31. Richard Glazar, in C. Lanzmann, *Shoah* (New York: Pantheon, 1985), p. 50.
32. The one exception was Crematorium IV which was blown up during an uprising by the Sonderkommando at Auschwitz on 7 October 1944.
33. C. Lanzmann, 'Le Lieu et la Parole' (*Cahiers du Cinema*, July–August 1985), in J. Robbins, 'The Writing of the Holocaust' (*Prooftexts* 1987, 7), pp. 249–58, p. 52.
34. R. Breitman, *The Architect of Genocide: Himmler and the Final Solution* (Bodley Head, 1991), p. 243.
35. Menachem Kon, 15.11.42, in J. Kermish (ed.), *To Live with Honor and Die with Honor! Selected Documents from the Warsaw Ghetto Underground Archive 'O.S.'* (Jerusalem: Yad Vashem, 1986), p. 24.

36. Levi, *The Drowned and the Saved*, p. 7.
37. C. Kaplan, *Scroll of Agony* (Hamish Hamilton, 1966).
38. E. Ringelblum, in D. Roskies (ed.), *The Literature of Destruction* (Philadelphia: JPS, 1989), p. 396.
39. Kaplan, *Scroll of Agony*, 26.10.39.
40. O. Singer, 27.7.42, in A. Adelson and R. Lapides (eds.), *Lodz Ghetto* (New York: Viking, 1989), p. 299.
41. Lanzmann, *Shoah*, pp. 103, 200.
42. S. Ezrahi, *By Words Alone* (Chicago: Chicago University Press, 1980), p. 15.
43. Kaplan, *Scroll of Agony*, 14.9.39.
44. Z. Gradowski, in Roskies (ed.), *The Literature of Destruction*, p. 548.
45. E. Ringelblum, *Notes from the Warsaw Ghetto* (New York: Schocken, 1974), pp. 295–6.
46. A. Wieviorka, 'Testimony' in G. Hartman (ed.), *Holocaust Remembrance* (Basil Blackwell, 1994), pp. 23–32, p. 31.
47. E. Wiesel, *Legends of Our Time* (New York: Schocken, 1982), p. 8.
48. Such memorials are to be found in Kazimierz, and in the Jewish cemeteries in Krakow and Warsaw. For a discussion of such memorials, see J. E. Young, *The Texture of Memory* (New Haven: Yale University Press, 1993), pp. 185–208.
49. J. E. Young, 'The Veneration of Ruins' (*Yale Journal of Criticism*, 1993, 6:2), pp. 275–83, p. 279.
50. G. Hartman, 'The Book of Destruction' in S. Friedlander (ed.), *Probing the Limits of Representation* (Cambridge, Massachusetts: Harvard University Press, 1992), pp. 318–34, p. 325.
51. P. Levi, *Moments of Reprieve* (Abacus, 1987), p. 10.
52. E. Wiesel, 'A Personal Response' (*Face to Face* 1979, 6), pp. 35–7, p. 36.
53. E. Wiesel, 'Why I Write' in I. Greenberg and A. Rosenfeld (eds.), *Confronting the Holocaust* (Bloomington: Indiana University Press, 1978), pp. 200–6, p. 206.
54. Stanislaw Krajewski comments on contemporary Jewish perceptions of Poland: 'Jews see Poland as a forsaken place where Jewish culture flourished a long time ago, then it got worse and worse, it all ended in tragedy, and there is now only a painful absence.' (In A. Bryk, 'Poland and the Memory of the Holocaust', *Partisan Review* 1990, 57:2, pp. 228–38, p. 233.)
55. L. Langer, *Holocaust Testimonies: The Ruins of Memory* (New Haven: Yale University Press, 1991), p. 52.
56. Ezrahi, *By Words Alone*, p. 110.

2

MYSTIFYING THE HOLOCAUST?

Given the amount written on the subject, terms such as 'incomprehensible', 'inexplicable', and 'ineffable' recur with surprising regularity in relation to the Holocaust. Many survivors and scholars remain adamant that the experience is essentially incommunicable. They argue that the Holocaust as '*l'univers concentrationnaire*', 'the Kingdom of Night', is unapproachable because it is a self-enclosed world that lies beyond our comprehension. Only those who were there can *know*. Those who were not there (the 'non-survivors') can only listen to and learn from those who were. According to such a view, the testimony of the survivors is essential because it provides the only access point to the alien world of 'over there'. Such a view lies behind the titles of books such as *Against Silence* and *Thinking the Unthinkable*. That such a view is widespread disturbs a number of scholars. This disquiet lies behind alternative titles such as *Against Mystification* and *Comprehending the Holocaust*. Thus it is apparent that there are two broad schools of thought. The first asserts that the Holocaust is ultimately incomprehensible, and therefore incommunicable. The second asserts that the Holocaust is as explicable as any other experience, and insists that it must be normalized through absorption into existing disciplines such as history or the social sciences. To the first group, calls for the normalization of the Holocaust fail to acknowledge its unique character and the challenge it represents. To the second group, emphasis upon the incomprehensibility of the Holocaust is potentially dangerous: it mystifies the event and threatens to place it beyond the scope of critical analysis. Each of these two positions will be considered in turn. Both approaches will then be analysed in terms of their understanding of a recurring theme in discussion of the Holocaust — silence.

—— *The Incomprehensibility of the* —— *Holocaust*

It was terrible. No one can describe it. No one can recreate what happened here. Impossible? And no one can understand it.[1]

Simon Srebnik's comment encapsulates the view that the Holocaust can be neither described nor understood fully. Such a view is common to both victims and survivors. At its most developed, as typified by the work of Elie Wiesel, this takes the form of asserting that there is something essentially mysterious about the events of the Holocaust. A number of victims recorded their doubts about their ability to do justice to the events they were attempting to describe. Chaim Kaplan observed that 'reality has outdone imagination'; Menachem Kon feared that 'the world will not be able to imagine a fraction of the atrocities'; for Jozef Zelkowicz, 'mere human language is too weak to relay what we see and hear'.[2] Many survivors hold similar views. Primo Levi referred to 'the ineffable universe of the camps'.[3] The reluctance and/ or inability of many survivors to speak forms a constant refrain in the film *Shoah*. The pressure Lanzmann exerted on obviously reluctant survivors to speak proved to be one of the more controversial elements in the film. Such pressurizing is at its most evident in an exchange between Lanzmann and Abraham Bomba after the latter had broken down in tears while giving his testimony:

B: I can't. It's too horrible. Please.
L: We have to do it. You know it.
B: I won't be able to do it.
L: You have to do it. I know it's very hard. I know and I apologize.
B: Don't make me go on please.
L: Please. We must go on.[4]

Part of the value of *Shoah* (and of video testimony) lies in the fact that it makes us acutely conscious of survivors' struggle to speak by incorporating the hesitancies and silences: 'unlike literary testimony, video testimonies can also represent *not* telling a story, the point at which memory will not enter speech.'[5] One of Lanzmann's strengths, both as a film-maker and as an interviewer, is that he is prepared to allow these silences to be heard, rather than interrupt the speaker or edit them out. He objected to the publication of a text of the film precisely because it omitted these hesitations and silences. It is no coincidence that while the film lasts 9 hours 23 minutes, the published text runs to under 200 pages. For Lanzmann, to present the text in this way is to miss the point of his film.[6] Silence and absence are central motifs: the silence of the victims, those who witnessed their fate, and the landscape itself. In reviewing the film, Amos Oz emphasizes the centrality of these twin motifs in Lanzmann's approach:

> The language of the film is the language of photographed silence; the language of pursed lips and gaping, speechless mouths; the language of never-ending freight trains, and the language of snowscapes of

barren fields. The dark green language of the Polish winter and the clear dazzling blue summer language of the Tel Aviv seashore.[7]

As well as questioning their ability to speak, a second preoccupation is evident in the testimony of a number of survivors: to what extent are *they* the true witnesses of the Holocaust? Most, if not all, who write on the Holocaust acknowledge that there is a qualitative difference in perspective between those who experienced these events first hand, and those who did not (although many would argue that this observation would apply to any experience, not simply the Holocaust). In addition, a number of survivors argue that there is an analogous difference in perspective between those who died and those who survived, with the only true witnesses being the dead. Somewhat surprisingly perhaps, this is a theme that runs throughout the work of Primo Levi. Although adamant that it *is* possible to speak of the Holocaust in a clear and comprehensible way, Levi is equally insistent that the testimony of survivors is 'a discourse on "behalf of third parties"', the story of things seen from close by, not experienced personally'.[8] Such a claim is built upon a sharp distinction drawn between 'the drowned and the saved' (the title of both a key chapter in his memoir, *If This Is a Man*, and his final book). The 'saved' are defined both positively and negatively. As a positive category, they are 'the few, the different', those who found 'the will and capacity to react'.[9] Understood in this sense, it is possible to be numbered among the 'saved' even if one did not survive. However, Levi also notes that 'the saved are not the ones that deserved salvation in the theological sense, but rather the shrewd, the violent, the collaborators.'[10] By way of contrast, the 'drowned' are an 'anonymous, faceless, voiceless mass'.[11] In the camps, the 'drowned' were those doomed to selection, known in camp slang as *muselmänner*:

> They, the *muselmänner*, the drowned, form the backbone of the camp, an anonymous mass, continually renewed and always identical, of non-men who march and labour in silence, the divine spark dead within them, already too empty to really suffer. One hesitates to call them living: one hesitates to call their death, death, in the face of which they have no fear, as they are already too tired to understand.[12]

For Levi, it is the 'drowned' who are the true witnesses, whereas the 'saved' are 'an anomalous minority'.[13] However, he contends that only the 'saved' have stories. To be able to tell one's own story requires a clear sense of identity, of individuality. It is symptomatic of a capacity to react. As we have seen, for Levi this is a characteristic of the 'saved', and he devotes *Moments of Reprieve* and *If Not Now, When?* to telling their stories. By contrast, it is of the very essence of the 'drowned' that they 'have the same story, or more exactly, have no story'.[14] They are anonymous, voiceless. Survivors are therefore confronted with a dilemma. On the one hand, they feel a compulsion to tell their own story and that of the 'drowned' to whoever is willing to listen. On the other hand, the story of the 'drowned', by its very nature, cannot be told. The core of the survivors' message is therefore incommunicable in so far as it presumes to relate the experience of the 'drowned' who have no story.

That such a view is held by Primo Levi, thought of by many as the most restrained and rational of commentators, indicates just how widespread is the view that the experience of the Holocaust ultimately lies beyond words.[15] Such a view is more often associated with Elie Wiesel who is viewed as the 'most eloquent and extreme exponent' of the mystification of the Holocaust.[16] According to Wiesel, the Holocaust is 'a sacred realm', 'a mystery begotten by the dead'.[17] As such it must be approached with 'fear and trembling'.[18] Only those who were there, the victims and survivors, can *know*. Wiesel echoes Levi in insisting that such knowledge can never be fully communicated. But according to Wiesel, the problem lies in the limitations of the descriptive capabilities of language, and in the non-survivor's inability to comprehend what is being so inadequately communicated: 'whoever has not lived through the event can never know it. And whoever has lived through it can never fully reveal it.'[19] For Wiesel, the Holocaust takes on mythological proportions. It bears witness to 'a confrontation between absolute sacredness and absolute impurity'.[20] Throughout his work, Wiesel is adamant that the Holocaust allows for only *three* possible roles: those of victim, perpetrator and bystander. However, the interpretation of the Holocaust as 'a confrontation between absolute sacredness and absolute impurity' tends to reduce this even further in allowing for only two diametrically opposed possibilities: the victims personify absolute innocence, while the perpetrators personify absolute evil. In such a mythological scenario, there is little conceptual space for the bystander. As a consequence, those who might be termed 'bystanders' either identify themselves with the victims, or are identified by others with the perpetrators (for further discussion of this point, see pp. 81–2).

It is precisely this tendency to mythologize that concerns Wiesel's critics: does it place the Holocaust beyond the scope of critical analysis by allowing a response solely of awe and reverential silence? One of the dangers inherent in Wiesel's approach is that it appears to exclude the possibility that the boundaries between victim, perpetrator and by-stander might, in some instances, become blurred. In his polemic essays (as opposed to his memoir, *Night*), the victims are identified with absolute innocence. Any approach (such as that of Hannah Arendt or Bruno Bettelheim) which seeks to analyse the behaviour of the victims is deemed unacceptable, precisely because it seeks to evaluate objectively.[21] For Wiesel, there can be no objectivity or detachment in relation to the victims: 'We must side with the sacred memories of those who died.'[22] Analysis is acceptable, indeed is to be encouraged, but only in so far as it seeks to increase understanding. It is unacceptable if it presumes to pass judgement on the behaviour of the victims.

Such a position raises the question as to where we draw the line between understanding and judgement. Critics suggest that approaches such as Wiesel's encourage the application of 'a sensitivity quotient' to the Holocaust which serves to exclude any discourse that goes beyond 'expressions of mourning and remorse'.[23] If such a criterion is to be applied, there is a danger that certain subjects will become taboo. The behaviour of the *Judenräte* (Jewish Councils) is an obvious case in point.[24]

—— Comprehending the Holocaust ——

Concern that critical analysis will either be limited or precluded generates much of the unease expressed at the mystification of the Holocaust, particularly as advocated by Wiesel. Critics point out that such an approach, even if unintentional, can serve to limit or stifle debate. It can also serve as an avoidance strategy by placing more complex or controversial issues (such as the behaviour of the victims) beyond the realm of critical analysis. Such critics are adamant that the Holocaust was a phenomenon in human history and, as such, is 'susceptible to understanding and explanation'.[25] This position is force fully argued by the philosopher Dan Magurshak in an essay, 'On the "Incomprehensibility" of the Holocaust: Tightening Up Some Loose Usage'. It finds more moderate expression in the work of the historians Yehuda Bauer and Michael Marrus.

Magurshak's article represents a detailed critique of the notion of incomprehensibility as it is often applied to the Holocaust by Elie Wiesel and others. Magurshak's central thesis is that 'the Holocaust is, in principle, as comprehensible and as amenable to disciplined study as any complex human phenomenon.' Those elements that are incomprehensible are not uniquely so: if they were unique, he suggests, then the incentive to analyse such events would be seriously compromised.[26]

For Magurshak, the assertion that the Holocaust is incomprehensible is primarily an affective or aesthetic response, an expression of revulsion, of being completely overwhelmed by the testimony of victims and survivors. However, such an emotional response does not logically entail the conclusion that the Holocaust is *theoretically* incomprehensible. Such an emotional response is common to other encounters with extreme horror, such as accounts of life in the trenches in the First World War. From this basis Magurshak proceeds to challenge the notion that only those who were there can *know*. While he willingly acknowledges that there is a difference between living through an experience and being a non-participant, however sympathetic, he again points out that this is not unique to the Holocaust but applies to any experience. In addition, it is generally accepted that the function of literature and film is to help us overcome this gulf by allowing us 'to enter into a new world and to experience it as if we had lived through it ourselves' – this, for example, was one of the assumptions underpinning Spielberg's decision to make *Schindler's List*.[27] Academic study also enables us to go part of the way towards overcoming this gulf in experience: what happened? where and why did it happen? Various causal chains can be deduced that suggest which particular combination of factors enabled the Holocaust to take place and develop in the way that it did. The more these events are studied by historians, psychologists and others, the more data will be collected. Magurshak concludes that, in principle: 'There is no good reason to deny that careful, exhaustive, historical, cultural and psychological studies will not, at least ideally, yield a complete and coherent account that traces the course of events and the play of factors by which the atrocity came about.'[28]

While agreeing with Magurshak's strictures against mystification, Bauer and Marrus are less confident that 'a complete and coherent account' can be achieved. Both insist that the Holocaust is explicable, and must be studied as such. For Bauer, the Holocaust is 'as explicable as any other series of violent acts in recorded history'.[29] For Marrus, it is essential 'to understand what happened to European Jewry as one would understand any other historical problem'.[30] Yet both historians are reluctant to suggest that this is equivalent to obtaining a 'complete and coherent account'. Bauer cautions, 'we can understand the Holocaust, not completely, not absolutely, but approximately'.[31] The challenge is to avoid mystification (understood negatively in the sense of 'to make obscure or secret') 'without destroying the mysterious quality that every historical event, and most certainly this one, possesses'.[32] For Marrus, it is essential that the historian retains a 'sense of limitation' because 'those separated from these events – either by chronology or historical circumstance – can never penetrate their horrors or grasp their ultimate significance.' He concludes that historians 'simply do the best we can, knowing that our efforts are necessarily imperfect, incomplete, and inadequate'.[33]

Are the views of Marrus and Bauer that far removed from those of Wiesel? Is it more a difference in approach, rather than a fundamental disagreement? Both historians call for the 'normalization' of the Holocaust within the general stream of historical understanding, and are adamant that it must be subject to critical analysis. Wiesel would not disagree, as long as the specifically Jewish aspects of the experience were acknowledged. The point of difference appears to be the choice of subject matter, and the tone and language adopted. Wiesel's primary concern is with the victims and survivors. He prefers to glorify rather than criticize them. Such a preference has given rise to criticism that he romanticizes the victims and survivors. However, such a strategy is a conscious choice: 'I am well aware that not all of them were by any means saints . . . I leave it to others to speak ill of them. For my part, I prefer to speak well.'[34] Having said this, it is necessary to distinguish between Wiesel's portrayal of the victims in *Night* and that in his polemic essays, 'A Plea for the Dead' and 'A Plea for the Survivors'. While the essays may be open to the charge that he romanticizes the victims, the same cannot be said of his memoir, *Night*.[35] Furthermore, it is interesting to note that Bauer specifically exempts Wiesel from his critique of mystification. He notes that Wiesel's 'mystical' approach is combined with a thorough knowledge of the academic literature on the subject.[36] Bauer suggests that the ideal approach to studying the Holocaust is one which accommodates both 'the soul-searing writings of those who were there' and the ever-burgeoning body of scholarly literature.[37] By relying solely on the latter, there is a danger of 'immersing tears and suffering in oceans of footnotes, of coming up with a remote quasi-scientific approach'.[38] However, such scholarly literature renders 'the soul-searing writings of those who were there' intelligible and meaningful by placing them in context. For Bauer, the ideal situation is one where the Chronicler (the academic community, and historians in particular) works, and is read, in conjunction with Job (the survivors).

What Can – and Cannot – Be Said [39]

The dispute over the (in)comprehensibility of the Holocaust is closely related to a second debate, namely whether silence constitutes the most appropriate response. The advocacy of silence rests on the assumption that the Holocaust is, in one sense at least, incomprehensible, and therefore beyond language.

As we have seen, many victims and survivors echo Jozef Zelkowicz' lament, 'No matter how much we write and tell, in the end we come up with but a pale reflection of reality.'[40] Neither should it come as a surprise to find that silence is a dominant motif in the work of Elie Wiesel, who remains adamant that the Holocaust 'by its very nature defies language'.[41] A variation upon this argument emerged in the course of the Carmelite controversy: one of the main objections to the nuns' presence was that silence, rather than institutional prayer, was the only appropriate way to remember the dead at Auschwitz. Many survivors and scholars argue that language is inadequate, occasionally even inappropriate, when confronted by the Holocaust. They often defend this position by citing T. W. Adorno's dictum that there can be no poetry after Auschwitz. The only language held to be appropriate is the faltering language of those who were there, the victims and the survivors. Such speech, however, often 'seems to testify to the futility of testimony itself'.[42] Just as the view that the Holocaust is incomprehensible has been challenged, so too has the advocacy of silence. Michael Marrus warns that such advocacy is 'a counsel of despair – yielding the field to falsification or oblivion'.[43]

It becomes evident that there is a variety of arguments underlying the advocacy of silence as an appropriate response to the Holocaust. These arguments, some of which have been outlined above, suggest that silence itself is a category that can be understood in various ways. For Marrus, it is symptomatic of apathy, evasion or irresponsibility. It indicates an unwillingness to assume the responsibility of speech, with all the pitfalls that speech may entail. In many ways, the appeal to silence suggests a longing for an ideal world, free of generalized, inaccurate, or distorted images of the Holocaust. Such a longing is understandable, if naive. Total silence is unattainable, as is evident from the ever-growing literature on the Holocaust. However, given that Wiesel is one of the most prolific writers on the subject, it would seem obvious that 'silence here is not identical with simple muteness'.[44] Rather silence can signify both a refusal to speak inappropriately and respect for the dead (as in the case of the Carmelite controversy), or silence can be interpreted as an expression of humility, of 'fear and trembling' when confronted by the 'sacred realm' of the Holocaust. For Wiesel, the advocacy of silence stems from an acute awareness of the limitations of language when confronted by the Holocaust. Just as Lanzmann makes a point of incorporating his witnesses' silences and reluctance to speak into his film, so Wiesel, by advocating silence, is indicating the complexity of speaking about the Holocaust.

Three primary strategies can be employed by way of response. The first aims to indicate the impossibility of communication. In *The Differend* Jean-François Lyotard notes that 'the silence that surrounds the phrase *Auschwitz was the extermination camp* is not a state of mind [*état d'âme*], it is a sign that something remains to be phrased which is not, something which is not determined.'[45] The inability or reluctance to speak indicates that there is something that 'remains to be phrased', and that what remains exceeds that which has been said. One example of the reluctance to speak which functions in this way is found in *Shoah*, in an exchange between Lanzmann and Mordedrai Podchlebnik. The two are talking about Simon Srebnik (Srebnik and Podchlebnik were the only survivors of Chelmno):

L: What died in him in Chelmno?

P: Everything died. But he's only human, and he wants to live. So he must forget. He thanks God for what remains, and that he can forget. And let's not talk about that.

L: Does he think it's good to talk about it?

P: For me it's not good.

L: Then why is he talking about it?

P: Because you're insisting on it.

The plea 'let's not talk about that' functions here as a way of beginning to talk, or at the very least serves to give some indication of the nature of what is not being said.[46]

A second (but related) strategy is to focus solely upon details, or upon stories that may appear to be tangential. By describing the 'how', it is possible to indicate the 'why'. This strategy can also be illustrated by reference to *Shoah*. Lanzmann continually asks his interviewees to describe the mechanics of the process of destruction: what was the weather like, how did they feel, what did the camp look like, how did the camps operate, and so on. His methodology is similar to that of the historian Raul Hilberg, the only non-participant interviewed in the film:

In all of my work I have never begun by asking the big questions, because I was afraid that I would come up with small answers; and I have preferred to address these things which are minutiae or details in order that I might then be able to get together in a gestalt a picture which, if not an explanation is at least a description, a more full description, of what transpired.[47]

Wiesel's methodology represents a slight variation upon this approach. With the exception of *Night* and his polemic essays, he addresses the subject indirectly. Rather than addressing the Holocaust as such, his novels either recreate pre-war *shtetl* life, or focus upon the aftermath and the survivors' struggle to rebuild their lives. In addition, Wiesel focuses upon subjects seemingly unrelated to the Holocaust: the Bible, Talmud and Hasidism.[48] However, in doing so he continues to explore the impact of the Holocaust:

> To avoid painful subjects, I explore others: Biblical, Talmudic, Hasidic or contemporary. I evoke Abraham and Isaac so as not to reveal the mystery of my relationship with my father. I recount the adventures of the Besht so as not to dwell on the fate of his descendants. In other words, I use literature to look away.[49]

For Wiesel, biblical figures function as archetypes: the story of Cain and Abel is the first genocide, Isaac is the first survivor, Jeremiah the first survivor-witness, and so on. On one level he is offering an analysis of the biblical text, on another he is searching for a way of responding to the Holocaust. For it is only in the light of the Holocaust that 'the full range of implications' in such texts becomes apparent.[50]

A third response is to identify criteria for judging what kind of speech is and is not appropriate in relation to the Holocaust. One possible approach is to insist that only those who were there (the survivors) have the right to speak. However, strict application of such a criterion would ensure that 'the Holocaust would die with the generation that went through it.'[51] While it is essential to heed 'the soul-searing writings of those who were there', such writings must be contextualized by reference to the available scholarly literature. For as Primo Levi himself points out, in some senses survivors had the worst vantage point as far as knowledge of the Holocaust was concerned.[52] Many became aware of the whole picture only after liberation.

An alternative and even more emotive criterion is proposed by Irving Greenberg when he suggests that 'no statement, theological or otherwise, should be made that would not be credible in the presence of burning children.'[53] However, the application of such a criterion would bring us full circle, for what statements would be 'credible' in such a context? Would not the consequence of any strict application of such a criterion be total silence? An additional question arises: who is to judge what would or would not be credible in such a context? There is a certain analogy here to Levi's insistence that the dead are the only true witnesses to the Holocaust. For, if Greenberg's criterion is to be applied seriously, then presumably only 'the burning children' are in a position to judge which statements are credible. As they are numbered among the dead, then no one is in a position to make that judgement for them: the result will again be silence. It would appear that all such criteria represent ideals. Can they also be interpreted as a reaction to what are deemed to be unacceptable responses to – or uses of – the Holocaust? The question of how, or indeed whether, we should evaluate such uses or misuses of the Holocaust will be discussed in the following two chapters.

NOTES

1. Simon Srebnik in C. Lanzmann, *Shoah* (New York: Pantheon, 1985), p. 6.
2. C. Kaplan, *Scroll of Agony* (Hamish Hamilton, 1966), 16.4.42; Kon, 1.10.42, in J. Kermish (ed.), *To Live with Honor and Die with Honor!* (Jerusalem: Yad Vashem, 1986), p. 86; Zelkowicz, 6.4.43, in A. Adelson and R. Lapides (eds.), *Lodz Ghetto* (New York: Viking, 1989), p. 385.
3. P. Levi, 'Revisiting the Camps' in J. E. Young (ed.), *The Art of Memory* (Munich and New York: Prestel-Verlag, 1994), p. 185.
4. Lanzmann, *Shoah*, p. 117. A number of reviewers criticized the 'relentless bullying of some of the victims' (review of *Shoah* in *Time* 4.11.85, p. 53). In Lenny Rubenstein's view, 'perhaps the most disturbing feature about *Shoah* is the stress to which Lanzmann subjects a number of his eyewitnesses'. ('*Shoah*', *Cineaste* 1986, 14:3, pp. 39–41, p. 41). By contrast, Ilan Avisar sees the same scene as 'one of the most memorable sequences in the history of cinematic representation' (*Screening the Holocaust*, Bloomington: Indiana University Press, 1988, p. 27). Young is somewhat ambivalent in his response to the scene. On the one hand, he describes it as 'one of Lanzmann's strikingly choreographed scenes'. On the other, he rhetorically asks: 'do we revictimize the survivors by forcing them to recreate experiences, to suffer them once literally and then again imaginatively now before our eyes?' (*Writing and Rewriting the Holocaust*, Bloomington: Indiana University Press, 1988, p. 168).
5. Young, *Writing and Rewriting the Holocaust*, p. 161. For a more detailed analysis of the significance of video testimony, see L. Langer, *Holocaust Testimonies* (New Haven: Yale University Press, 1991).

   As well as incorporating hesitancies and silences, *Shoah* also includes all stages of translation on screen. For Young, 'the effect at times is that of a multilingual echo-chamber, in which experiences seem to be in search of a language.' (*Writing and Rewriting the Holocaust*, p. 160).

6. Lanzmann was highly critical of the published text of *Shoah*. He told one interviewer, 'There are silences in the film but these have been eradicated in the book, thereby altering the whole tone.' (V. Dignam, 'An Unforgettable Canvas of Events', *Morning Post* 6.2.87).

7. A. Oz, *The Slopes of Lebaanon* (Vintage, 1991), p. 162.

8. Levi, *The Drowned and the Saved*, p. 64. Earlier in the book, he notes that 'the history of the Lagers has been written almost exclusively by those who, like myself, never fathomed them to the bottom.' (p. 6).

9. Levi, *Moments of Reprieve*, p. 10.

10. Levi, in a letter to Alvin Rosenfeld, 15.9.85, cited in A. Rosenfeld, 'Primo Levi: The Survivor as Victim' in J. S. Pacy and A. P. Wertheimer (eds.), *Perspectives on the Holocaust: Essays in Honour of Raul Hilberg* (Boulder: Westview, 1995), pp. 123–44, p. 139.

11. Levi, *Moments of Reprieve*, p. 10.

12. Levi, *If This Is a Man* (Abacus, 1987), p. 96.

13. Levi, *The Drowned and the Saved*, pp. 63–4.

14. Levi, *If This Is a Man*, p. 96.

15. For example, writing in the *Daily Telegraph*, David Jones described Levi as 'one of the best, most articulate, and most moving of the witnesses to Auschwitz precisely because his testimony is not an outraged accusation; it is controlled, detached, even ironic.' (8.9.91).

16. A. Lerman, 'The Art of Holocaust Remembering' (*Jewish Quarterly* 1989, 135), pp. 24–32, p. 24.

17. I. Abrahamson (ed.), *Against Silence: The Voice and Vision of Elie Wiesel*, 3 Volumes (New York: Holocaust Library, 1985), Vol. 1, p. 190; Wiesel, *One Generation After*, p. 43.

18. E. Wiesel, *A Jew Today* (New York: Vintage, 1979), p. 237.

19. Wiesel, *A Jew Today*, p. 234.

20. Abrahamson (ed.), *Against Silence*, Vol. 1, p. 362.

21. See: H. Arendt, *Eichmann in Jerusalem: A Report on the Banality of Evil*, Revised and Enlarged Edition (Penguin, 1965); B. Bettelheim, *On Surviving and Other Essays* (Thames & Hudson, 1979).

22. Abrahamson (ed.), *Against Silence*, Vol. 1, p. 367.

23. P. Lopate, 'Resistance to the Holocaust' (*Tikkun* 1989, 4:3), pp. 55–65, p. 59.

24. Much of the debate surrounding Arendt's reports on the Eichmann Trial centred on her comments on the *Judenräte*. See: H. Arendt, *The Jew as Pariah* (New York: Grove Press, 1978), pp. 240–79; D. Barnouw, 'The Secularity of Evil' (*Modern Judaism* 1983, 3), pp. 75–94; B. Bettelheim, 'Eichmann: The System, the Victims' (*New Republic* 1963-4, 148), pp. 23–33; J. Robinson, *And the Crooked Shall Be Made Straight* (New York: MacMillan, 1965).

25. Lerman, 'The Art of Holocaust Remembering', p. 27.
26. D. Magurshak, 'On the "Incomprehensibility" of the Holocaust: Tightening Up Some Loose Usage', in A. Rosenberg and G. Myers (eds.), *Echoes from the Holocaust* (Philadelphia: Temple University Press, 1988), pp. 421–31, p. 422.
27. Magurshak, 'On the "Incomprehensibility" of the Holocaust', p. 425.
28. Magurshak, 'On the "Incomprehensibility" of the Holocaust', p. 427.
29. Y. Bauer, 'Holocaust and Genocide: Some Comparisons' in P. Hayes (ed.), *Lessons and Legacies* (Evanston: Northwestern University Press, 1991), pp. 36–46, p. 36.
30. M. Marrus, *The Holocaust in History* (Weidenfeld & Nicolson, 1988), p. 6.
31. Y. Bauer, 'Conclusion: The Significance of the Final Solution' in D. Cesarani (ed.), *The Final Solution* (Routledge, 1994), pp. 300–9, p. 304.
32. Y. Bauer, *The Holocaust in Historical Perspective* (Sheldon Press, 1978), pp. 47, 30.
33. Marrus, *The Holocaust in History*, pp. 6–7.
34. De Saint-Cheron and Wiesel, *Evil and Exile*, pp. 15–16.
35. Lawrence Langer suggests that the 'sentimentality' that characterizes passages in Wiesel's polemical essays should be regarded as 'the momentary lapse of a stubbornly clear-sighted intelligence'. See: Langer, 'The Divided Voice', in Greenberg and Rosenfeld (eds.), *Confronting the Holocaust*, pp. 31–48, pp. 35–6.
36. Bauer, *The Holocaust in Historical Perspective*, pp. 45–6.
37. Bauer, *The Holocaust in Historical Perspective*, p. 49.
38. Bauer, *The Holocaust in Historical Perspective*, p. 5.
39. For a more detailed analysis of silence and the limits of language in relation to the Holocaust, see my essays: 'What Can – and Cannot – Be Said: Religious Language after the Holocaust' (*Literature and Theology* 1992, 6:1), pp. 47–56; and 'Religious Language after the Holocaust', in F. Young (ed.), *Dare We Speak of God in Public?* (Mowbray, 1994).
40. Zelkowicz, in Adelson and Lapides (eds.), *Lodz Ghetto*, p. 385.
41. Wiesel, *A Jew Today*, p. 48.
42. A. Rosenfeld, 'Jean Améry as Witness', in Hartman (ed.), *Holocaust Remembrance*, pp. 59–69, p. 68.
43. Marrus, *Holocaust in History*, p. 7.
44. D. LaCapra, 'Representing the Holocaust' in Friedlander (ed.), *Probing the Limits of Representation*, pp. 108–27, p. 111.
45. J. F. Lyotard, *The Differend* (Manchester University Press, 1988), pp. 56–7. For current discussion of language and the Holocaust, see: M. Blanchot, *Writing the Disaster* (Lincoln: University of Nebraska Press, 1986); B. Lang (ed.), *Writing and the Holocaust* (New York: Holmes &

Meier, 1988), pp. 154–99; M. Lustigman, *Kindness and the Art of Reading Ashes* (New York: Peter Lang, 1988).

46. Lanzmann, *Shoah*, p. 7. For a discussion of this theme in *Shoah* see D. Carroll, 'Foreword. The Memory of Devastation and the Responsibilities of Thought: "And Let's Not Talk about That" ' in J. F. Lyotard, *Heidegger and 'the jews'* (Minneapolis: University of Minneapolis, 1990), pp. vii–xxix.

47. Lanzmann, *Shoah*, p. 70.

48. See, for example, E. Wiesel, *Messengers of God* (New York: Summit Books, 1976), and *Sages and Dreamers* (New York: Touchstone, 1991).

49. E. Wiesel, *From the Kingdom of Memory* (New York: Summit Books, 1990), p. 143.

50. Wiesel, *Messengers of God*, pp. xiii–iv.

51. Bauer, *The Holocaust in Historical Perspective*, p. 45.

52. While recognizing the importance of the testimony of survivors, Levi insists that it must be approached critically: 'For knowledge of the Lagers, the Lagers themselves were not always a good observation point. In the inhuman conditions to which they were subjected, the prisoners could barely acquire an overall picture of their universe.' (*The Drowned and the Saved*, p. 6).

53. I. Greenberg, 'Cloud of Smoke, Pillar of Fire', in E. Fleischner (ed.), *Auschwitz: Beginning of a New Era?* (New York: KTAV, 1977), pp. 7–55, p. 23.

3

FORMS OF REMEMBRANCE I: MEMORIALIZING THE HOLOCAUST

Remembrance of the Holocaust assumes a variety of forms: testimony, research, education, film, literature, liturgy, support for the State of Israel, and so on. It can also be reified in memorials and museums. The debate generated by such memorials and museums serves as a microcosm of the wider debate surrounding the use and misuse of the Holocaust. The current proliferation of Holocaust memorials is particularly controversial in view of the fact that some of these sites are now major tourist attractions. Today, as Jack Kugelmass notes, we need to address the question of 'Holocaust tourism'.[1] Recent estimates suggest that there are 600,000 visitors a year to Auschwitz; 300,000 to Maidanek; 900,000 to Dachau; 600,000 to the Anne Frank House in Amsterdam; 1,250,000 to Yad Vashem; and 350,000 to Beit Hashoah (the Museum of Tolerance) in Los Angeles. Prior to opening, the staff of the USHMM in Washington DC expected 750,000 visitors in the first year. In the event, more than 623,000 visited the Museum between 22 April and 2 October 1993 (20,000 in the first week, 70,000 in the first month).[2] Why are visitors coming to these places in such numbers, and what are they seeing when they get there? Is 'Holocaust tourism' yet one more manifestation of what some fear is the commercialization and/or trivialization of the Holocaust? Alternatively, is such interest a sign of hope for the future, a concrete example of a worldwide commitment to remembrance? Or is it a combination, in varying degrees, of the two?

—— Memorializing the Holocaust ——

The activity of Holocaust memorialization takes place first between events and memorials, then between memorials and viewers, and, finally, between viewers and their lives in the light of the memorialized past.[3]

The variety of motivations for remembering the Holocaust is reflected

35

in the diversity of memorials, and the explanations given for building them. Some are inspired by the belief that subsequent generations must be educated in order to guard against any repetition in the future. Such museums serve as a repository of memory, one that their founders hope will gain in importance as the generation of survivors dies out. Others are dedicated to those who died, and stand as a concrete witness to what was destroyed. Just as bearing witness serves as a 'tombstone to the dead', so too can the building of memorials. Michael Berenbaum suggests that: 'One reason that memorials are built to the Holocaust is because we feel compelled to produce something concrete to commemorate a world that disappeared. . . . Memorials are being built as an inadequate response to an overpowering sense of loss.'[4] Thus, memorials and museums function as one more weapon in the struggle to defeat the Nazis' 'war against memory': they stand as a permanent reminder of what was intended to be an 'event without a witness'.[5] By erecting plaques or building memorials on the sites of destruction, the desire that the Holocaust would be 'an unwritten and never to be written page of glory' is, in theory at least, permanently thwarted.

By building memorials or preserving material remains, survivors (or the community as a whole) hope to etch the memory of events into the landscape, thereby forcing it to bear witness so that either a trace of what took place remains, or that there is a memorial counter-assertion that what was destroyed is not forgotten. If nothing more, the absence of those who died or the events that took place at a particular site are recorded and commemorated. Claude Lanzmann's inclusion of extensive footage of the memorial stones at Treblinka in *Shoah* provides one example of how memorials can function in this way: 'The stones were for me the killed Jews, the human beings. I had nothing else to film except the stones, and I filmed them with such a feeling of emergency that they became for me the human beings and that they have become now for the viewers the human beings.'[6] Such an approach will succeed only if the viewers, or the visitors to these sites, are aware of – or interested in – the significance of what they see. As time passes, the likelihood is that such markers will themselves merge into the landscape – in much the same way as the numerous war memorials dotting the European countryside often pass unnoticed, other than on Remembrance Day, except by those with a personal link, such as veterans or relatives of those who died.[7]

Building memorials serves to provide a focus of mourning for both the individual and the community. Many of those who died have no known grave or date of death. As a consequence, any attempt to remember the victims of the Holocaust carries an inherent danger of abstraction, as, for example, in the use of 'six million' as a synonym. Many attempts to memorialize the Holocaust strive to reverse this process by commemorating individuals (for example, the statue of Mordechai Anielewicz at Yad Mordechai in Israel), communities (a number of the memorial stones at Treblinka), or events (the memorial at the Umschlagplatz, the site of deportations from the Warsaw Ghetto). At Auschwitz, plaques have been donated commemorating individuals who died. Many visitors to the site leave flowers, national flags or candles on the ruins of the gas chambers and crematoria at Birkenau, or at the Wall of Death in Auschwitz-I.

Yad Vashem, Israel's Martyrs' and Heroes' Remembrance Authority, serves as an illustration of how memorializing the Holocaust performs a variety of functions. Established by the Knesset in 1953, Yad Vashem stands as 'the monument of a nation's grief'.[8] Mandated by law to be both 'custodian and creator of national memory' of the Holocaust, the Authority was charged with responsibility for research, the collation of testimony, and perpetuating the memory of both the victims and the 'communities, organizations and institutions which were destroyed because they were Jewish'.[9] To carry out these duties, Yad Vashem includes a historical museum, archives, and a research and teaching centre. Relatives and friends are encouraged to register the names of those who died in 'Pages of Testimony' (to date, over three million names have been recorded and filed in the Hall of Names). Publications include Pinkhas Hakehilot (Encyclopedia of Destroyed Communities), the aim of which is 'to record and describe the history of over 5,000 annihilated communities'.[10] The Avenue of the Righteous perpetuates the memory of more than 8,600 individuals designated 'Righteous among the Nations' for risking their lives on behalf of Jews during the Holocaust. The numerous memorials dotted around the complex include the Valley of the Destroyed Communities; a Monument commemorating the Jewish Community of Czerniakov; and Korczak and the Children of the Ghetto. The Wall of Remembrance (a replica of Nathan Rapoport's Warsaw Ghetto Uprising memorial) serves as the backdrop for the annual state remembrance service on Yom Hashoah (Holocaust Remembrance Day). However, in spite of the evident determination to remember particular individuals, communities and events, abstraction remains an inevitable part of such memorialization, and is at its most obvious in the initial division of the victims into the twin categories of 'Martyrs' and 'Heroes'.

In view of the ever-increasing number of memorials, and the diverse motivations for remembrance, it is perhaps inevitable that there should be a heated debate concerning the memorialization of the Holocaust. Andreas Huyssen notes the 'multiple fracturing of the memory of the Holocaust in different countries'.[11] Memorials in Israel focus upon the motifs of 'Martyrs and Heroes', 'Holocaust and Heroism': the emphasis is upon the Holocaust as the culmination of Diaspora existence, and proof of the need for a strong, independent Jewish state.[12] In Poland, the emphasis is either upon loss and dislocation (roughly 90 per cent of Poland's Jews were killed), or the Holocaust is seen as a figure for the suffering of the Polish nation (as in the controversial use of the figure six million to depict Polish losses: three million ethnic Poles and three million Polish Jews). As early as 1947, Auschwitz and Maidanek were designated monuments to 'the Martyrdom and Struggle of the Polish and Other Nations'.[13] In the United States, the story told is one of the victory of democracy and pluralism over intolerance and indifference: 'the Jew functions as a true American symbol – in the popular sense – of hope and the promise of America.'[14] Such variety of interpretation is equally apparent in the choice of memorial inscriptions: 'Earth conceal not the blood shed on thee' (Bergen-Belsen); 'Remembrance is the key to redemption' (Yad Vashem); 'Zakhor/Remember' (Philadelphia); 'For the dead and the living we must bear witness' (USHMM); 'Never again' (Treblinka); 'Our fate is a warning to you' (Maidanek).

Such plurality can generate unease: are memorials vulnerable to revisionism and exploitation? Are they of value only in so far as their meaning is unambiguous? The difference between the views of Harold Marcuse and James Young is instructive. Marcuse argues that the value of memorials lies in direct proportion to the accuracy and sufficiency of the information they convey: 'Monuments should contain enough specific and personal information, including the identification of the perpetrators' and the victims' names, to anchor the injustice in public consciousness.'[15] For Young, this is to misunderstand the function of memorials: by its very nature, a memorial is ambiguous. The meaning generated may differ depending on the preconceptions of those who visit it, and the context within which it is viewed. He argues that memorials are essentially dialogical: 'It is not to Holocaust memorials as such that we turn for remembrance, but to ourselves within the reflective space they both occupy and open up. In effect, there can be no self-critical monuments, but only critical viewers.'[16] Thus, the meaning of any memorial may vary as it reflects the conceptions of those viewing it. For example, the memorial at Auschwitz-Birkenau may suggest one meaning when functioning as the backdrop for a papal mass celebrated by a Pole, John Paul II, and quite another when providing the focus for a gathering of survivors or the March of the Living.

The recent preoccupation with building Holocaust memorials and museums is also challenged on other grounds. Three criticisms predominate. First, are too many being built? Nearly every major city in the United States has built, or is in the process of building, at least one Holocaust memorial. Before long there will also be three major Holocaust museums (Los Angeles, Washington DC and New York). Is this an appropriate use of resources, or should the money be spent elsewhere, for example on education or the provision of counselling support for survivors and their children? Second, is the Holocaust coming to dominate Jewish self-consciousness to an unhealthy degree? Jacob Neusner goes so far as to speak of 'Holocaustomania', and refers to contemporary American Judaism as the 'Holocaust memorial movement' (such views will be further considered in the following chapters). Third, do such memorials misrepresent or distort the individuals and communities they purport to remember? Often, Jews are depicted solely as victims: the focus is upon how Jews died, rather than the values by which they lived. It is perhaps inevitable that memorials, and particularly museums, will focus upon the events of 1933–45. As has been noted, the victims are often known solely through the artefacts they left behind, or photographs (taken primarily by the Nazis themselves). While attempts are made to highlight the victims' perspective, this can all too often be submerged by that of the perpetrators.

Even those in favour of building memorials recognise the validity of such criticisms, at least to a certain extent. Supporters are divided as to where such memorials should be located: the sites where events took place? in Israel? wherever there is a sizeable Jewish community? Should such memorials remember only the fate of the Jews, or should they include reference to the fate of other victims of the Nazis, such as Gypsies, homosexuals, Jehovah's Witnesses, and Soviet prisoners-of-war? Should parallels be drawn with events such as the Armenian genocide or the current situation in the former Yugoslavia? These are just some of the issues preoccupying those attempting to memorialize the Holocaust.

—— Auschwitz: Memorializing the —— Holocaust in Situ

'When people say "Holocaust", they think of Auschwitz.'[17] As this statement suggests, Auschwitz has come, for many, to be synonymous with the Holocaust. Given its symbolic importance, the question of how the site should be preserved and utilized is much debated. Writing in *The Times* in April 1991, Roger Boyes concluded:

> There are three dangers for the future. The first is that Auschwitz will in some way be politicized. The second is that the camp will become a religious battleground, with Christians and Jews arguing over what is, in effect, the world's largest graveyard. And, finally, there is a risk that the myth of Auschwitz will somehow swamp the historical facts.[18]

Even in 1991, the suggestion that these are 'three dangers for the future' was an expression of unwarranted optimism. The politicization of Auschwitz was inevitable from the moment that it was designated a 'Monument to the Martyrdom and Struggle of the Polish and Other Peoples'. This process was further exacerbated by the decision to establish a series of pavilions dedicated to the experience of different national groups. The Carmelite controversy (1985–93) is indicative of the fact that the site already is 'a religious battleground'. Furthermore, the battleground is not a solely religious one. Many of the controversies surrounding Auschwitz can be interpreted as disputes over the symbolic ownership of the site: conflict is rooted in the existence of very different interpretations of 'the historical facts'.

Both the emergence of Auschwitz as the ultimate symbol of the Holocaust, and the use of the term 'Auschwitz' itself, are suggestive of mythologization. Outside of Poland, the German 'Auschwitz' has supplanted the Polish 'Oświęcim' as the accepted designation of the site. Strictly speaking, it is a generic term encompassing a complex that covered 15 square miles and included three main camps: Auschwitz-I, Auschwitz-II (Birkenau), and Auschwitz-III (Buna-Monowitz). The 1947 resolution designating Auschwitz as a 'Monument to the Martyrdom and Struggle of the Polish and Other Peoples' also included the provision that a Museum be established on the site. This Museum, located in Auschwitz-I, is run under the auspices of the Polish Ministry of Culture. In 1989, the then Prime Minister, Tadeusz Mazowiecki, established the International Auschwitz Council to consider appropriate ways of commemorating the events that took place there.

During the course of recent controversies, it has become apparent that Auschwitz is popularly viewed as one undifferentiated mass. Little significance is attached to either its geographical construction or its historical evolution. Auschwitz today is as much 'a place of the mind, an abstraction, a haunted idea' as it is a physical reality.[19] As a consequence, 'the physical encounter with Auschwitz today can be a fundamentally disorientating experience.'[20] For some, the physical reality of Auschwitz today – with its tourists, souvenir shops, and increasing proliferation of memorials – is more than disorientating: it detracts from or blurs the intrinsic, symbolic meaning. The reason why many visitors, including survivors, prefer Birkenau is precisely because fewer people visit it, and it has been left relatively untouched (unviolated?) by restoration in comparison to Auschwitz-I. Consequently, or so it seems, at Birkenau the visitor is confronted by fewer distractions. For others, the meaning of Auschwitz lies precisely in the encounter with physical reality: 'There is no substitute for a visit to the camps. No book, no film can convey the intensity of standing where unspeakable events took place.'[21] Such a viewpoint raises the question of what precisely we do encounter in Auschwitz. Are we encountering the physical relics of the Holocaust, or a subtle combination of original artefacts and restoration? The fact that we are encountering the latter has been cited by revisionist historians as 'proof' that there were no gas chambers, that the Holocaust itself is a 'hoax'. For example, the gas chamber and crematorium in Auschwitz-I were reconstructed in 1948 (the original having been turned into an air-raid shelter by the Nazis, and then destroyed by the Soviets).[22] In addition, barbed wire fences, fence posts, chimney stacks, railway tracks, watch-towers and wooden barracks have all been restored. Is such restoration appropriate? Should there be full reconstruction? Or should the site be left to decay gradually? Such questions take on increasing urgency in view of the deteriorating condition of the site, and the raising of $20 million by the Lauder Foundation for the purpose of conservation. How should such money be spent, and who should decide?

Not surprisingly, there are many views on the subject, not least among the staff of the State Museum and the International Auschwitz Council. A series of conferences and symposia have been held which serve to reflect the spectrum of views. One suggestion by the Museum staff is that display boards 1.6 metres high should be erected in Birkenau with descriptions and photographs of what took place there. In addition, notices should be posted indicating the location of crematoria and mass graves with a request that such sites be treated with respect. A further proposal is that the 'Sauna' should be restored and turned into a memorial, displaying the plaques donated in memory of those who died.[23] The historian Yaffa Eliach suggests that a reconstructed cattle-car should stand on the ramp at Birkenau. Jean-Claude Pressac argues that the gas chamber and Crematorium II should be reconstructed. James Young, meanwhile, believes that the site should be left as it is. Yet another approach is that of Jonathan Webber, who argues that priority should be given to the establishment of a Jewish memorial at Birkenau, possibly in the Field of Ashes.[24] Such a spectrum of views serves to indicate the complexities inherent in memorializing the Holocaust *in situ*. The controversy generated by the USHMM indicates the problems surrounding memorializing the Holocaust at a distance from the sites of destruction.

The United States Holocaust Memorial Museum (USHMM)

On 1 November 1978, President Carter established a Commission on the Holocaust, with Elie Wiesel as chairperson. In 1980, Congress unanimously passed a resolution establishing the United States Holocaust Memorial Council, and charged it with the creation of a 'living memorial'. When the Council determined that this memorial should take the form of a museum, the State donated a plot of Federal land 400 yards from the Washington Memorial adjacent to the National Mall.[25] The cost of the project ($168 million) was raised through private donations. The Museum was formally opened by President Clinton on 26 April 1993, in front of ten thousand people, including numerous visiting dignitaries. The opening of the Museum coincided with the fiftieth anniversary of the Warsaw Ghetto Uprising (on 19 April) and the week-long Days of Remembrance (19–25 April). The Museum itself is a complex containing a permanent exhibition; a Hall of Remembrance; film, photo and video archives; a research institute; 80,000 files of the American Gathering of Holocaust Survivors; and an interactive learning and resource centre for teachers. According to Harvey Meyerhoff, Chairperson of the Holocaust Memorial Council from February 1987 to May 1993, the intention is: 'that all visitors to the Museum will leave not just with knowledge, but with the determination to speak out and act against injustice and racism and the denial of basic human rights, and to make that commitment part of their lives.'[26]

From the moment of its inception, the Museum generated controversy. At the planning stage, the historian Lucy Dawidowicz, a Council member, publicly disassociated herself from the decision to build a museum rather than a memorial.[27] There was public disagreement over an appropriate definition of the Holocaust. It was ultimately decided that the Museum would be devoted to the fate of the Jews, but would highlight the uniqueness of the Holocaust by contextualizing it within the Nazis' treatment of other groups.[28] From the start, the validity of the entire project was questioned: why build a national museum of the Holocaust in the civic heart of the United States, particularly given that there was no equivalent museum dedicated to the experience of slavery or the treatment of native Americans?[29] Supporters of the Museum reacted by arguing that America was an immigrant society and, as such, the Holocaust was part of its history. For others, given the United States' self-understanding as the guardian of the free world, there could be no more appropriate location for a Holocaust museum: the Holocaust becomes the ultimate violation of the Bill of Rights. According to Stuart Eizenstat, former Chief Domestic Policy Advisor to President Carter, the Museum is justified on historical and political grounds: 'It was the US that led the allied effort to defeat the Nazi war machine and that liberated the death camps of Europe. . . . No country in the world has America's particular concern for human rights and has embodied it in its politics at home and abroad.'[30] Critics continued to express concern at such an 'Americanization' of the Holocaust: would it descend into kitsch? Particular concern was expressed at the decision to name individual sections of the Museum, with the exception of the permanent exhibition and the Hall of Remembrance, after major donors.

Those involved with memorial projects elsewhere were worried about possible financial repercussions. Both the Auschwitz State Museum and Yad Vashem are government funded and chronically under-resourced. Their supporters were concerned as to whether they could compete with the institutions emerging in the United States, either financially or technologically. Were these new institutions to be seen as complementary, or as competition? The USHMM insists that its role is complementary, but some of its supporters seem less sure. Charles Krauthammer, for instance, argues that an American Holocaust Museum is not only desirable, it is essential:

> Yes, there are Holocaust memorials in Poland and elsewhere. But these are not to be trusted. Who knows what Europe, birthplace of the Nazi plague, will one day say or do with these monuments . . .
>
> Yes, there is a memorial in Israel. One might say that Israel itself is a memorial to the Holocaust. But there will be those in generations to come who will not trust the testimony of the Jews.
>
> With this building, America bears witness. The liberators have returned to finish the job. First rescue, then remembrance. Bless them.[31]

Those engaged in planning the USHMM's exhibits were acutely conscious of the difficulties inherent in memorializing the Holocaust. Jeshajahu Weinberg, the director of the Museum, outlines the approach adopted: 'The Museum does not undertake to explain *why* the Holocaust happened . . . The Museum restricts itself meticulously to answering the question of *how* it happened, i.e. to presenting the well-established actual course of events.'[22] Beginning with the reactions of American troops entering the camps, the Permanent Exhibition falls into three distinct sections. The first, 'The Assault', charts the period 1933–39. The second, 'The Holocaust Years', portrays life in the ghettos, the activities of the *Einsatzgruppen*, the death camps, and resistance. The third, 'Bearing Witness', introduces the activities of Righteous Gentiles, and charts the attempts of survivors to build a new life either in Israel or the United States. Visitors are left to reach their own conclusions as to *why* these events took place.

In the Exhibition, there is a great reliance on artefacts. Of 30,000 acquired, 5,000 are on permanent display. These include a railroad car; an original barrack from Birkenau; cobblestones from the Warsaw Ghetto; one of the milk-cans used to hide the archive, *Oneg Shabbat*; a gate from the Jewish cemetery at Tarnow; a hand-cart from Theresienstadt; stones from the quarry at Mauthausen; camp uniforms, and a boat used in the rescue of Danish Jews in 1943. Given this predominance of artefacts, it is inevitable that much of the Exhibition portrays the victims from a Nazi perspective. In order to counteract this tendency, audio and video testimony is available, and emphasis is placed upon examples of spiritual and armed resistance.

In addition, the design of the Museum incorporates two bridges: the Bridge of Names, etched with 5,000 first names of victims of the Nazis, and the Bridge of Villages etched with the names of 5,000 destroyed communities. On arrival, each visitor is given an identity card telling the story of one particular individual. As the visitor proceeds through the Museum, they gradually learn more concerning the story of that one individual. The hope is that 'by personalizing the history, it comes within our grasp', and, as a result, visitors will identify with the victims rather than the perpetrators.'[33] Arguably the most powerful attempt to 'personalize' this history is found in the three-storey Tower of Faces, a collection of more than 1,300 photographs taken of the inhabitants of Ejszyszki, a *shtetl* in Lithuania, between 1900 and 1941. The majority of the inhabitants were shot on 25 and 26 September 1941. Only 29 survived. The Tower of Faces strives to represent 'the Jewish lives that were and are no longer', so that by focusing on 'the fate of one community we learn the fate of others'.[34]

—— *The future?* ——

Given the continuing controversy over how we should remember the

Holocaust, it is perhaps inevitable that commentators have begun to speak of the politics of commemoration. Memorializing the Holocaust has become highly politicized. Whether it will continue to be so remains to be seen. Will such sites increase or decrease in relevance once survivors are no longer with us? Perhaps these sites will gradually fade into the background, indistinguishable from the landscape of which they are a part, with the majority of the population unaware of what took place there. Or, perhaps, as intended, these memorials and museums will ensure that the memory of the Holocaust will indeed live on, long after those who witnessed it have died. What is already apparent is that the politics of commemoration is highly selective: what is remembered, and where, does not always happen 'naturally', and often it depends upon the intervention of influential individuals or groups. Thus, while Auschwitz, Dachau and the Anne Frank House are 'tourist attractions', other sites such as Belzec and Chelmno are rarely visited. The example of Plaszow, a concentration camp in the suburbs of Krakow, is perhaps instructive in this respect. Until recently, few visited Plaszow. Those who did visit would find relatively little to see: the camp was destroyed. On the site, there are two memorials. The site itself was not 'advertised', as were visits to nearby Auschwitz. However, since the release of *Schindler's List* (much of which is set in Plaszow), an increasing number of visitors are coming to the site. Indeed, one entrepreneur in Krakow now advertises 'Schindler Tours' to locations featured in the film. Will what is remembered of the Holocaust in the future depend as much, if not more, upon popular culture, than it will upon museums such as Auschwitz, Yad Vashem, and the USHMM?

NOTES

1. J. Kugelmass, 'Why We Go To Poland: Holocaust Tourism as Secular Ritual' in J. E. Young (ed.), *The Art of Memory: Holocaust Memorials in History* (Munich and New York: Prestel-Verlag, 1994), pp. 175–83.
2. The figure for Auschwitz is cited by Kazimierz Smolen, in J. Webber and C. Wilsack (eds.), *Auschwitz: A History in Photographs* (Bloomington: Indiana University Press, 1993), p. 263. The figures for Maidanek, Dachau, the Anne Frank House, Yad Vashem and Beit Hashoah are from J. E. Young, *The Texture of Memory* (New Haven: Yale University Press, 1993), p. x. The figures for the USHMM are from the Museum's newsletter, *Update* (November/December 1993), p. 2.

For a general discussion of Holocaust memorials, see: S. Milton, *In Fitting Memory: The Art and Politics of Holocaust Memorials* (Detroit: Wayne State University Press, 1991); Young, *The Texture of Memory*, and Young (ed.), *The Art of Memory*.

3. J. E. Young, 'The Art of Memory' in Young (ed.), *The Art of Memory*, pp. 19–38, p. 21.

4. M. Berenbaum, *After Tragedy and Triumph* (CUP, 1990), p. 50.

5. S. Felman and D. Laub (eds.), *Testimony: Crises of Witnessing in Literature, Psychoanalysis, and History* (Routledge, 1992), pp. 75–92.

6. Claude Lanzmann, cited in Felman and Laub (eds.), *Testimony*, pp. 256–7.

7. See, for example, G. Dyer, *The Missing of the Somme* (Hamish Hamilton, 1994), pp. 19, 68–76.

8. Abba Eban, cited in R. Dafni (ed.), *Yad Vashem*, Fifth Edition (Jerusalem: Yad Vashem, 1990), p. 2.

9. Young, *The Texture of Memory*, p. 246; Martyrs' and Heroes' Remembrance (Yad Vashem) Law, 5713–1953, cited in Dafni (ed.), *Yad Vashem*, p. 4.

10. Dafni (ed.), *Yad Vashem*, p. 34.

11. A. Huyssen, 'Monument and Memory in a Postmodern Age' in Young (ed.), *The Art of Memory*, pp. 9–17, p. 15.

12. For a more detailed discussion of Israeli memory of the Holocaust, see: S. Friedlander, 'The Memory of the *Shoah* in Israel' in Young (ed.), *The Art of Memory*, pp. 149–57; T. Segev, *The Seventh Million* (New York: Hill and Wang, 1993), pp. 419–517; Young, *The Texture of Memory*, pp. 209–81.

13. For a more detailed discussion of Polish memory of the Holocaust, see: K. Gebert, 'The Dialectics of Memory in Poland' in Young (ed.), *The Art of Memory*, pp. 121–9; R. Gruber, *Upon the Doorposts of Thy House* (New York: John Wiley & Sons, 1994), pp. 133–236; Young, *The Texture of Memory*, pp. 113–208.

14. J. Doneson, *The Holocaust in American Film* (Philadelphia: JPSA, 1987), p. 151. For a more detailed discussion of memory of the Holocaust in the United States, see: I. Avisar, *Screening the Holocaust* (Bloomington: Indiana University Press, 1988), pp. 90–133; Berenbaum, *After Tragedy and Triumph*, pp. 3–16; J. Miller, *One, by One, by One: Facing the Holocaust* (Weidenfeld & Nicolson, 1990), pp. 220–75; Peter Novick, 'Holocaust Memory in America' in Young (ed.), *The Art of Memory*, pp. 159–65; Young, *The Texture of Memory*, pp. 283–349.

15. H. Marcuse, 'West German Strategies for Commemoration' (*Dimensions* 1988, 3:2), pp. 13–14, p. 14.

16. J. E. Young, *Writing and Rewriting the Holocaust* (Bloomington: Indiana University Press, 1988), p. 189.

17. Doneson, *The Holocaust in American Film*, p. 173. For more detail concerning the current debate on the future of Auschwitz, see: 'The Yarnton

Declaration of Jewish Intellectuals on the Future of Auschwitz' (*European Judaism* 1990, 23:2), pp. 43–5; R. Boyes, 'Why Auschwitz Must be Saved' (*The Times* 24.11.93); R. Caseby, 'Echoing Footsteps' (*Sunday Times* 28.1.94); D. Cesarani, 'Preserving a Death Camp' (*The Guardian* 29.11.93); A. Uttley, 'The Auschwitz Horror Show (*Times Higher Educational Supplement* 21.8.92); C. Tyler, 'The Future of Auschwitz' *Financial Times* 5–6.2.94; J. Webber, *The Future of Auschwitz* (Oxford Centre for Postgraduate Hebrew Studies, 1992); Webber, 'Personal Reflections on Auschwitz Today' in Webber and Wilsack (eds.), *Auschwitz*, pp. 281–91; J. E. Young, 'The Future of Auschwitz' (*Tikkun* 1992, 7:6), pp. 31–3, p. 77.

18. R. Boyes, 'The Dying of the Light' (*The Times Saturday Review* 6.4.91), pp. 10–11, p. 10.

19. Young, *The Texture of Memory*, p. 142.

20. Webber, 'Personal Reflections on Auschwitz Today', in Webber and Wilsack (eds.), *Auschwitz*, pp. 284–5.

21. H. Muschamp, 'Shaping a Monument to Memory' (*New York Times* 11.4.93).

22. D. Dwork and R. J. van Pelt, 'Reclaiming Auschwitz' in G. Hartman (ed.), *Holocaust Remembrance* (Basil Blackwell, 1994), pp. 232–51, pp. 238–41.

23. Teresa Świebocka, in conversation with the author, Auschwitz State Museum, 27.5.93.

24. Cesarani, 'Preserving a Death Camp'; Webber, *The Future of Auschwitz*, pp. 26–8.

25. For a discussion of the significance of this topography, see: C. Griswold, 'The Vietnam Veterans' War Memorial and the Washington Mall' (*Critical Inquiry* 1986, 12), pp. 688–719; Young, *The Texture of Memory*, p. 338.

26. Cited in USHMM Newsletter, Special Issue (Summer 1993), p. 2.

27. Miller, *One, by One, by One*, p. 258.

28. See Berenbaum, *After Tragedy and Triumph*, pp. 17–32.

29. See, for example, P. Gourevitch, 'In the Holocaust Theme Park' (*Observer Magazine* 30.1.94), pp. 20–5, p. 24. For more detail on the controversy generated by the USHMM, see: H. M. Belitsky, 'Memory and Accidental Tourists' (*Hadassah Magazine* 1993, 74:8), pp. 26–9; B. Gill, 'The Holocaust Museum: An Unquiet Sanctuary' (*New Yorker* 19.4.93), pp. 107–9; Miller, *One, by One, by One*, pp. 230–6, 251–66; L. Wieseltier, 'After Memory' (*New Republic* 2.5.93), pp. 14–26; Young, *The Texture of Memory*, pp. 335–47.

30. S. Eizenstat, 'Holocaust Memorial Deserves Capital Place' (*Together* June 1993), p. 18.

31. C. Krauthammer, 'Holocaust Museum: Where Infamy Achieves Immortality' (*Washington Post* 23.4.93).
32. Jeshajahu Weinberg, in M. Berenbaum, *The World Must Know* (Boston: Little, Brown & Company, 1993), pp. xiv–xv.
33. Berenbaum, *The World Must Know*, p. 235.
34. 'The Ejszyszki Shtetl Collection' in Berenbaum, *The World Must Know*.

4

FORMS OF REMEMBRANCE II: THE HOLOCAUST IN POPULAR CULTURE

'Holocaust tourism' is a relatively recent phenomenon, and one that stands in sharp contrast to the original response – or lack of response – to these events. Apart from a number of accounts by survivors, relatively little was written about the Holocaust in the immediate aftermath of the war. The term 'Holocaust' itself only became widely used during the 1960s, having first appeared in the *New York Times* on 30 May 1959.[1] This initial lack of interest in the subject is evident in the inconspicuous beginnings of two texts now widely regarded as classics of Holocaust literature. Several Dutch publishing houses rejected the *Diary of Anne Frank* before it was finally published in 1947 with a limited run of 1,500. The same year marked the publication in Italy of Primo Levi's memoir, *If This Is a Man*. Only 2,300 copies were printed, many of which remained unsold. The situation gradually began to change in the 1960s. The turning points were the capture and trial of Adolf Eichmann (1960–1) and the Six Day War (1967). The Eichmann trial generated worldwide interest, and Hannah Arendt's coverage sparked off intense debate, both over her thesis that Eichmann embodied 'the banality of evil', and her views on the behaviour of the *Judenräte*. Haim Gouri suggests that in Israel the trial gave survivors of the Holocaust a platform from which to speak of their experiences: 'overnight, they became the focus of attention.'[2] For Tom Segev, 'the trial served as national group therapy', enabling Israelis to confront the immediate past as embodied by the survivors.[3] The Six Day War had a similar impact. In the tense days leading up to the war, many spoke of their fears of a second Holocaust.[4]

From this point onwards, relative silence gave way to burgeoning interest. The Holocaust became the subject of an ever-increasing number of books, plays and films. In one sense, this interest reached its apex in April 1978 with the broadcast on four consecutive evenings of *Holocaust: The Story of the Family Weiss*. The popular success of *Holocaust* introduced the subject to a mass audience. Yet, for many critics, such success was symptomatic of a worrying trend. Previously, the concern had been that few were interested in the Holocaust. The ratings success of *Holocaust* suggested that this was no longer the case (the same could also be said of *Schindler's List*). Yet in both cases, critics have questioned the meaning of such success: what kind of knowledge is being communicated? Today, it seems that 'the problem is no longer "never to forget": it is how to remember.'[5] Titles such as 'The Use and Misuse of the Holocaust', 'Exploiting Atrocity' and 'Trivializing Memory' reflect this growing unease. Such articles express concern at both the quantity and the quality of many representations of the Holocaust, and argue that past neglect has given way to excess. Such articles warn of the dangers of commercialization, sensationalism and trivialization. It is suggested that the current preoccupation with the Holocaust is excessive, even morbid: people learn how Jews died, not of the values by which they lived. The question arises as to whether mere exposure to the subject is sufficient. What kind of knowledge or awareness of the Holocaust is being disseminated? Such discussion is all the more pressing given that 'in a few more years, the flesh-and-blood witnesses will be gone. All that will remain are written or recorded traces, images.'[6]

—— *The Holocaust in Popular Culture* ——

Since the mid 1970s the Holocaust has become marketable. It is now part of mainstream popular culture and, as such, is 'fair game for writers, novelists, historians, theologians and philosophers with different backgrounds and unequal skills'.[7] Such interest generates its own problems. Are there any popular uses of the Holocaust that are unacceptable or invalid? If so, who is in a position to make such a judgement, and upon what grounds? Two broad responses emerge in response to such questions. The first is a purist approach: its advocates are adamant that it is both possible and necessary to distinguish between 'authentic' and 'inauthentic' representations of the Holocaust. The second approach is more populist and acknowledges that the Holocaust is now fair game for anyone who wishes to address it. Advocates of the latter approach suggest that 'inauthentic' representations of the Holocaust are a regrettable but inevitable by-product of the fact that these events are now 'firmly entrenched as a public image of reference'.[8]

A purist approach to representation begins with the assumption that the Holocaust is unique. The testimony of victims and survivors is granted privileged status, for only those who were there can truly *know*. There is an assumption that the Holocaust is incomprehensible, and ultimately beyond language. Any response must therefore begin with an acknowledgement of its own limitations: if victims and survivors question their capacity to describe the events they experienced, how can anyone else presume to imagine or recreate them? For the purist, any approach to the Holocaust must be characterized by humility and respect, even reverence.

Inevitably, perhaps, Elie Wiesel is one of the strongest advocates of a purist stance:

> The Holocaust is not a subject like all the others. It imposes certain limits. There are techniques that one may not use, even if they are commercially effective. In order not to betray the dead and humiliate the living, this particular subject demands a special sensibility, a different approach, a rigour strengthened by respect and reverence and, above all, faithfulness to memory.[9]

As examples of representations that transgress these limits, Wiesel cites films (*The Night Porter, Seven Beauties, Sophie's Choice*); plays (Joshua Sobol's *Ghetto*); and television series (*Holocaust, War and Remembrance*). By way of contrast, those deemed 'authentic' include accounts written by victims of the Holocaust (Chaim Kaplan, Emmanuel Ringelblum); documentaries (*Shoah, Night and Fog*); and the work of historians (Raul Hilberg, Lucy Dawidowicz, Martin Gilbert, Michael Marrus). It is significant that whereas the vast majority of positive examples are factual, all those held to be unacceptable are fictional, and by non-survivors. While favouring a documentary approach, Wiesel concedes that some films do 'succeed in moving us without lapsing into cheap sentimentality', and, as examples, cites *The Garden of the Fitzi Continis* and *The Shop on Main Street*.[10] It should be noted, however, that neither of these films was a mainstream commercial success.

Ironically, even Wiesel's list of 'authentic' representations is more inclusive than some. While many would agree with his evaluation of *Night and Fog* (1955), others would argue that it is 'inauthentic'. According to the director, Alain Resnais, 'the constant idea was to not make a monument to the dead, turned to the past.' Rather, the intention was to show that 'if this existed, it could happen again; it exists now in another form.'[11] He hoped that his audience would be inspired to draw parallels with French policy in Algeria and American involvement in Vietnam. In order to highlight the universal ramifications of the subject, the film does not highlight the particularity of Jewish suffering under the Nazis, and for this reason, a number of critics argue that the film should be deemed an 'inauthentic' representation of the Holocaust.[12]

For Wiesel, 'inauthentic' approaches to the Holocaust are characterized by a lack of reverence for their subject matter. *Night and Fog* cannot be faulted in this respect. The script is by a survivor, Jean Cayrol, and the tone of the film is meditative, even elegiac. Wiesel argues that this is precisely where *Night and Fog* differs from more popular treatments of the Holocaust. The former dazzles with its authenticity, the latter 'profane and trivialize a sacred subject'.[13] Such a lack of reverence often takes the form of a determination to show everything, either in words or pictures. 'Inauthentic' representations of the Holocaust are undermined by their very confidence in the capacity of the mass media to communicate. Dramas such as *Holocaust* attempt to reconstruct and incorporate all the essential elements of the experience: in so doing, there is an inevitable danger of over-simplification. For Wiesel, all 'inauthentic' representations are characterized by 'false certainties and arrogance'.[14] He is willing to admit that popular treatments of the Holocaust succeed in reaching a wide audience, but doubts the accuracy, even integrity, of the knowledge being disseminated. As a consequence, they are 'an outrage to the memory of the dead, and to sensitivity'.[15] By contrast, those cinematic treatments of the Holocaust that are acceptable 'don't purport to show everything': their 'authenticity' lies in direct proportion to the humility and restraint shown.[16] For Wiesel: 'One does not imagine the unimaginable. And in particular one does not show it on screen.'[17]

Similar views are voiced by the literary critic, Alvin Rosenfeld. Like Wiesel, he believes that the only 'authentic' representations are those that approach the Holocaust with awe. Reverence is the appropriate response when confronted by an experience that undermines the very capacity of language to communicate. Rosenfeld shares Wiesel's preference for the work of victims and survivors and suggests that, other than novels by survivors, the only 'authentic' creative response to the Holocaust is found in the poetry of Paul Celan and Nelly Sachs. He suggests their poetry bears witness to the 'expiration' of speech in the face of such an experience.[18] Most other creative representations are dismissed as 'inauthentic' on the grounds that they fail to meet the demands of historical accuracy. To be deemed 'authentic', a fictional representation of the Holocaust must be judged against 'a particularly careful standard of truth'.[19] In this context, there can be no artistic licence to create, or to imagine. Reality is such that any attempt to recreate these events creatively is doomed to failure. As a consequence, Rosenfeld echoes Wiesel in concluding that many plays and films about the Holocaust rely on clichés, and thus present 'a cartoon version of life and death' in the ghettos and camps.[20]

If there is a key criterion of 'authenticity' for Rosenfeld, it lies in a commitment to the uniqueness of Jewish suffering in the Holocaust. The clearest indication of 'inauthenticity' is any tendency to generalize or universalize. As examples, he cites Peter Weiss' play, *The Investigation*; William Styron's novel, *Sophie's Choice*; and Sylvia Plath's poems, 'Daddy' and 'Lady Lazarus'. *The Investigation* is based upon the Auschwitz War Crimes Trials held in Frankfurt am Main (1964–5). Weiss made no secret of the fact that his purpose in writing the play was to highlight the universal significance of Auschwitz: '*The Investigation* is about the extreme abuse of power that alienates people from their own actions. It happens to be German power, but that again is unimportant. I see Auschwitz as a scientific instrument that could have been used by anyone to exterminate anyone.'[21] In order to emphasize the fact that Auschwitz symbolizes a universal human problem, the word 'Jew' is never mentioned in the play, despite its subject matter. For Rosenfeld, such an omission serves only to depersonalize the victims. Weiss' approach is 'inauthentic' because it ignores, or chooses to overlook, the specificity of Jewish experience of the Holocaust. Rather, Auschwitz is utilized as a vehicle for a more generalized attack on the evils of capitalism. For Rosenfeld, 'to see Auschwitz in such terms is, of course, not to want to see it at all.'[22]

Although William Styron interprets the Holocaust in very different terms to Weiss, Rosenfeld's critique of *Sophie's Choice* runs along similar lines. The eponymous heroine of the novel is a survivor of Auschwitz, yet Styron identifies her as a Polish Catholic. Furthermore, he states that Sophie 'had suffered as much as any Jew who had survived the same afflictions, and had in certain profound ways suffered more than most'.[23] For Rosenfeld, the suggestion that a Polish Catholic could have 'in certain profound ways suffered more' than the Jewish victims of Auschwitz is abhorrent. Such 'inauthenticity' is further compounded by the fact that much of the novel is set in post-war America, and describes Sophie's subsequent suffering at the hands of her Jewish lover, Nathan, with whom she ultimately dies in a suicide pact. For Rosenfeld, such a reversal of roles profanes the memory of the dead. Having said this, Styron's decision to make Sophie a Polish Catholic survivor of Auschwitz seems designed to provoke precisely this kind of reaction.

In addition, Rosenfeld accuses Styron of exonerating the true oppressors, namely the Nazis.[24] He objects vehemently to the sympathetic portrayal of the Commandant of Auschwitz, Rudolf Höss, and the fictional camp doctor, Fritz Jemand von Niemand (loosely based upon Josef Mengele). In presenting Höss and Jemand von Niemand in this way, Styron was influenced by Arendt's thesis of the banality of evil. His intention was to show that the Nazis were not monsters, but rather were 'human like you and me'.[25] For both Rosenfeld and Wiesel, however, such a portrayal is an abdication of moral responsibility, a blurring of the distinction between the absolute innocence of the victims and the absolute evil of the perpetrators.

Rosenfeld's third example of 'inauthenticity' is Sylvia Plath's two poems 'Daddy' and 'Lady Lazarus'. In both poems Plath employs the imagery of the Holocaust. 'Lady Lazarus' includes the verse:

> A sort of walking miracle, my skin
> Bright as a Nazi lampshade,
> My right foot
> A paper weight,
> My face a featureless, fine
> Jew linen.[26]

For Rosenfeld, this is 'to manipulate the language of the Holocaust for private ends'.[27] He is adamant that it is illegitimate to employ such a specific historical referent to an individual's private pain.

Thus the gulf separating purist and populist approaches to the representation of the Holocaust becomes apparent. The purist regards the Holocaust as sacrosanct, as a subject to be approached with reverence and trepidation. A populist approach differs in acknowledging that the Holocaust is now entrenched as a public image of reference. As such, there is nothing to prevent any writer or film-maker who wishes to do so from addressing the subject. A populist approach is, at root, a serious attempt to address the fact that 'more frequently than not, it is the least successful films in the eyes of the critics that exert the strongest influence on the public.'[28] The purist is idealistic, whereas the populist is pragmatic. For the purist, the Holocaust is sacrosanct: it must be protected from representations that are unworthy of it. To describe an approach as 'inauthentic' is to condemn it as inaccurate and/or inappropriate. When Rosenfeld accuses Sylvia Plath of manipulating 'the language of the Holocaust for private ends', he is suggesting that her appropriation of concentration camp imagery is inappropriate and, consequently, minimizes or denigrates the experience of those whose suffering was all too real. By contrast, a populist approach takes a more pragmatic line. James Young suggests that the choice is between excluding the Holocaust from public consciousness by placing it off limits, and accepting that as a public image of reference it is fair game for whoever wishes to address the subject: 'better abused memory . . . than no memory at all'.[29]

Rosenfeld and Wiesel may or may not be correct in labelling certain representations as 'inauthentic'. The fact remains that, short of censorship, there is little that can be done to prevent such 'inauthenticity'. Representations of the Holocaust vary greatly in terms of quality and style. A populist approach suggests that there is no way of legislating as to which approaches are acceptable and which are not. Once any representation enters the public domain it becomes subject to criticism. Only at this point does it become appropriate, if one so wishes, to differentiate between 'authentic' and 'inauthentic' representations of the Holocaust. To take *Sophie's Choice* as an example: Styron gave a number of interviews explaining his intentions at the time of the novel's publication. Some critics praised the book, while others (such as Rosenfeld) criticized it. Styron, in turn, defended his position. A similar process accompanied the release of the film. Individuals could then choose whether they wished to read the novel or see the film, and to reach a conclusion – if sufficiently interested – as to whether this treatment of the Holocaust is 'authentic' or 'inauthentic'.

Other defences of a populist approach to representation are possible. Does an artist have 'the right to use even the death camps as a metaphor, to reimagine or reinvent them to suit his or her own vision'?[30] Rosenfeld and Wiesel would say no, Styron would say yes. The former would argue that the Holocaust is sacrosanct and unique: 'There are no metaphors for Auschwitz, just as Auschwitz is not a metaphor for anything else.'[31] Styron dissents, and insists that the Holocaust is *not* sacrosanct. As subject matter, it is as available as anything else to the creative writer: there is no reason to claim 'that just because a person has experienced something it makes them a better artistic witness'.[32] The artist is free to exercise his or her imagination. If this were not the case, then there would be no such thing as a historical novel. Styron insists that he is entitled to employ the Holocaust as a metaphor for absolute evil. While careful to state that he is not writing from the perspective of a survivor, he insists that his approach is valid nevertheless: 'I have another vision, another metaphor, and I'm offended by the idea that somehow the metaphor of Sophie being forced to choose to murder one of her children is not a perfectly valid use of the Holocaust.'[33] The suggestion that there is a 'valid use' of the Holocaust highlights the gulf between Styron on the one hand, and Rosenfeld and Wiesel on the other. For the latter, the Holocaust is an event that confronts and challenges both artist and audience. It is not something that can be 'used' by the artist for his or her own purposes, however well intentioned these might be.

—— Holocaust ——

The screening of *Holocaust* prompted a worldwide debate over the representation of these events. According to its critics, the series cheapened its subject. For Claude Lanzmann, '*Holocaust* perpetrates a lie, a moral crime; it assassinates memory.'[34] Wiesel was equally harsh, dismissing the series as 'untrue, offensive, cheap'.[35] Others were equally vehement in their support. The American Jewish Committee gave the programme makers its Institute of Human Relations Media Award. According to the citation, *Holocaust* was 'without question the most effective dramatization yet presented on national television of the meaning of the Nazi era for the whole of mankind'.[36] In assessing the programme's impact in West Germany, Siegfried Zielinski suggested that 'because of the TV series the word "Holocaust" passed into the common language.' It is widely accepted that reaction to *Holocaust* played a significant role in influencing the West German government to reverse its decision to introduce a statute of limitations on Nazi war crimes.[37]

While the artistic and educational merits of *Holocaust* are hotly disputed, its commercial success is beyond question. First broadcast in April 1978, the seven-and-a-half-hour series was seen by 120 million Americans. It was nominated for sixteen Emmys, and won eight. When broadcast in West Germany in January 1979, it was watched by 15 million viewers, and was preceded and followed by a nationwide debate. Within a short period of time, the series had been seen by 220 million people in fifty countries. Such worldwide success was seen as vindication by the programme's supporters, while confirming the worst fears of its critics. Why was it that 'a clumsy story had broken through barriers of unawareness that more sophisticated assaults had not penetrated', and what kind of awareness was it that *Holocaust* generated?[38]

Even an arch-critic such as Elie Wiesel accepts that 'to attract a large public, you have to use a language it can understand' and adds, 'some concessions are necessary, perhaps even permissible, if the end is a good one.'[39] The question is: does *Holocaust* fall into this category? For Wiesel, the answer would obviously be no. For others, such as Judith Doneson and Clive James, the answer would be yes. No one denies that *Holocaust* contains factual errors. Many would concede that the strategy of telling the story of the Holocaust through the experience of two families is simplistic. Opinions differ as to whether this is an acceptable narrative device, or cheapens and distorts the Holocaust. Supporters argue that the device is justified because it personalizes the abstract statistics of mass murder. Doneson goes further, suggesting that 'whether or not the Weisses, or even the Dorfs, are true characters is unimportant, for they could have been – and that is what counts.'[40] Such a comment highlights the differences between the programme's supporters and its critics. The former argue that, while far from ideal, *Holocaust* succeeds in representing events in a manner which, despite minor inaccuracies, is essentially accurate. Critics counter by arguing that the series sanitizes, and thereby fundamentally distorts, the Holocaust. The picture it gives is therefore essentially misleading, if not false. In the words of Lawrence Langer, 'The failure of *Holocaust* is a failure of imagination. The vision which plunges us into the lower abysses of atrocity is not there.'[41] Others dismiss *Holocaust* as 'simplistic and emotionally manipulative', or as 'soap opera'.[42]

It cannot be denied that *Holocaust* relies upon simplifications, even stereotypes. There is much that can be criticized in the series, both on factual grounds and in terms of taste. However, it would be wrong to identify popularization and commercial success with trivialization. Many of those who adopt a purist stance tend automatically to assume that any commercially successful portrayal of the Holocaust must, by definition, be unacceptable. Part of the problem lies in the fact that such success reflects a 'secularization of what for so long was treated as a holy subject'.[43] Nowhere was this more obvious than in the decision by the American networks to intersperse *Holocaust* with commercial breaks. It is arguable that the critical as well as commercial success of *Schindler's List* was rooted in the fact that it succeeded in combining commercial success with an emphasis on the sacrosanct nature of the subject. Thus Spielberg avoided the taboo of secularization. However, even his reverential approach failed to appease a number of purist critics who remain resolute in their opposition to any popular representation of the Holocaust.

—— Shoah *and* Schindler's List ——

Whereas *Holocaust* was, on the whole, much maligned, *Schindler's List* proved to be a near-universal critical success – a fact reflected in the award of seven Oscars. The commercial and critical success of the film led the *Jewish Chronicle* to name Spielberg its 'Newsmaker of the Year', on the grounds that he had produced 'what is likely to become the single most lasting and powerful record' of the Holocaust.[44] This view was echoed in many of the critical responses to the film. Writing in the *New Yorker*, Terrence Rafferty described *Schindler's List* as 'by far the finest, fullest dramatic [i.e. non-documentary] film about the Holocaust'.[45] For Brian Cheyette, it was 'unquestionably, the best film on the subject within its particular set of conventions'.[46] However, the qualifications in such praise are significant. For Rafferty, *Schindler's List* is the finest 'non-documentary film'. For Cheyette, it is the best film on the subject 'within its particular set of conventions'. Such qualifications suggest an awareness of purist unease at the very idea of there being a popular film on the Holocaust. It is significant that the few negative reactions to *Schindler's List* all stress the problems inherent in representing the Holocaust within a popular medium. Furthermore, many go on to contrast the film unfavourably with Lanzmann's *Shoah*.

For many, *Schindler's List* exemplifies a populist approach to representation, whereas *Shoah* embodies a purist approach. A typical example of the debate over the worth of *Schindler's List* is a letter to the *Times Literary Supplement* dissenting from Brian Cheyette's favourable review. In his letter, Alan Gross argues that 'the point is surely not that the film is a flawed masterpiece . . . but that no popular film on the Holocaust should have been made because no popular film *can* be made.'[47] A subsequent letter in support of this view suggests that 'what's wrong with the film is essentially what is wrong with all popular culture, namely that its means of expression are debased and debasing.'[48] The basis of the objections to *Schindler's List* lies in the purist contention that popular culture is an inappropriate vehicle for representation of the Holocaust because it inevitably resorts to simplification and cliché.

Criticism of the film tends to echo that of *Holocaust*. First, Spielberg is criticized for daring to show what cannot be shown on screen. Objections are especially vociferous to the recreation of the gas chambers at Auschwitz, and in particular the scene where the women among the *Schindlerjuden* are unsure until the very last minute as to whether they are in a gas chamber or a shower.[49] Second, the film is criticized for its intrinsic optimism, and its failure to show the true horror of the Holocaust. *Schindler's List* focuses on those Jews who survived, and upon the role played by the exercise of personal moral responsibility in bringing this about. A typical critique is that of Simon Louvish:

> Spielberg and Keneally's Auschwitz is made comprehensible by the coherence of its narrative. There is, even in this hell, a happy ending . . . Even this can be endured. Survival seems a matter not of chance, but of the consequences of a *good deed*. Despite the horror, a comforting reassurance.[50]

Such a view finds some support in the ending of the film (with its comparison between the number of *Schindlerjuden* and their descendants, and the number of Jews in Poland today). Such a view is also encouraged by a number of statements by Spielberg, such as his assertion that 'each and every one of us, now or in the future, could be an Oskar Schindler. Each and every one of us has the duty to say: "Never again".'[51]

Those who criticize *Schindler's List* tend to contrast it unfavourably with *Shoah* – 'the only film on the Holocaust worth watching', according to Alan Gross.[52] They suggest that *Shoah* is a work of art, and, as such, avoids the excesses of popular culture. Such a comparison has been promoted assiduously by Lanzmann himself. He accuses Spielberg of turning the Holocaust into an 'adventure story' and suggests that 'to tell the story of the Holocaust through a German who saved Jews can only lead to a distortion of the truth because, for the overwhelming majority of the Jews, things did not happen like this.' Lanzmann sharply contrasts his own approach to that of Spielberg: '*Shoah* is a film about the destruction of the Jews. And *Schindler* is a film about the saving of the Jews. If so many people wanted to save the Jews, why did so many die?' He is also critical of Spielberg's attempt to represent as much of the Holocaust as possible. By way of contrast, Lanzmann insists that *Shoah* is marked by 'a real refusal to represent', and can be understood only as 'a fight against the impossibility to represent, to reconstruct'. His major objection is that Spielberg takes *Shoah* and then presumes to illustrate it. By doing so, *Schindler's List* undeniably presents the subject in a way that is more appealing to the general public. Lanzmann pre-empts this response by countering: 'I know one of the arguments is that people will learn something. That the film is a vehicle of communication. But *what* will they learn?'[53]

Lanzmann's objections echo those of Wiesel and Rosenfeld concerning *Holocaust* and *Sophie's Choice*. It is therefore not surprising to find that defences of *Schindler's List* follow similar lines. Marcel Ophuls may well be justified in describing *Shoah* as 'the greatest documentary about contemporary history ever made, bar none, and by far the greatest film . . . about the Holocaust'.[54] But it is also 9 hours 27 minutes long, and has only ever been seen by a limited audience. *Schindler's List* runs for 3 hours 16 minutes and, while longer than the average feature film, has been seen by millions of people world-wide. Spielberg's film has succeeded in attracting a mass audience, whereas Lanzmann's did not, even when shown on television. The question then arises: *what* are these millions learning when they see *Schindler's List*? Supporters of the film argue that it does indeed serve an important educational function. Writing in the *Sunday Times*, Susan Ellicott suggests that 'the power of entertainment is such that Spielberg might have done as much as the Jewish activist, Simon Wiesenthal, to prevent the Holocaust slipping from people's consciousness.'[55] The *Jewish Chronicle* concurs, hence its decision to name Spielberg as 'Newsmaker of the Year'. Staff at the USHMM argue that 'the Spielberg film has undoubtedly contributed to the massive upsurge in public interest in the Holocaust.'[56] Staff suggest that there is a direct correlation between the success of *Schindler's List* and the increasing numbers of visitors to the USHMM. If this assumption is correct, then it would seem that even if Spielberg's film is simplistic or partial in its account of the Holocaust, it has nevertheless served as the catalyst for a significant increase of interest in the subject. It is thus serving an educational purpose.

As far as the interpretation of the Holocaust in *Schindler's List* is concerned, Spielberg readily concedes that 'no film can ever show the Holocaust in all its true evil. It can never be told.'[57] However, he suggests that his approach is valid: the story of Oskar Schindler serves as 'a window', 'a sample of what it was like'.[58] Given that the film is based upon a true story, such an approach is reasonable enough, as indeed is Lanzmann's. What is important is to remember that neither approach tells the *whole* story; rather each sheds light upon a part of the whole. Spielberg's film is about a Righteous Gentile and those he enabled to survive. *Shoah* is about the machinery of destruction, and the continuing impact of the Holocaust upon those who experienced it. Rather than seeing the two films as mutually exclusive, it is perhaps more appropriate to see them as different versions of the Holocaust. For as Young observes when discussing Holocaust testimony:

> Each telling adds new dimensions both to the events and to our understanding of them and their effects on the prisoners themselves. Each version establishes a different set of moral implications, a different frame of critical reference; each raises new questions and is witness to a different act: of resistance, of rage, of courage, of revenge, or of desperation.[59]

Given such a variety of testimony to the Holocaust, it is perhaps inevitable that there should be an equal range of cinematic representations.

In the immediate aftermath of the war, there may well have been (in principle at least) a choice: either to speak of the Holocaust in order to reach as wide an audience as possible, or to remain silent. Many survivors decided to speak. As a consequence, the Holocaust is now established as a public image of reference – there is no going back. Given the nature of many representations of the Holocaust, it is perhaps understandable that there is a preference expressed in some quarters for a respectful silence. However, in view of the current situation, this is no longer a serious option. Rather than condemn all popular representations of the Holocaust, we need to ask why it is that they, rather than more 'authentic' responses, have succeeded in capturing the public's interest. The key question is whether *Holocaust* and *Schindler's List* serve as the means to a beneficial end. It could be argued that both, in their very different ways, succeed in translating the experience of the Holocaust into a language that can be readily understood. Such popular representations of the Holocaust exist *alongside* other approaches to the subject – those of historians, philosophers and theologians, as well as those of victims and survivors. In many cases, it is the initial interest generated by popular representations that creates sufficient interest for some of the audience to pursue other, perhaps less easily accessible approaches to the Holocaust. Ideally, the two approaches will have a symbiotic relationship: the former generating interest in the latter, and the latter re-presented in a distilled or simplified version in the former. Undoubtedly, there have been, and will continue to be, 'misuses' of the Holocaust. However, as we have seen, critics are alert to such dangers, both real and imagined.

NOTES

1. L. Jick, 'The Holocaust: Its Use and Abuse within the American Public' (*Yad Vashem Studies* 1981, 14), pp. 303–15, p. 309.
2. H. Gouri, 'Facing the Glass Booth' in G. Hartman (ed.), *Holocaust Remembrance* (Basil Blackwell, 1994), pp. 153–60, p. 154.
3. T. Segev, *The Seventh Million: The Israelis and the Holocaust* (New York: Hill & Wang, 1993), p. 351.
4. See, for example, the comments of Michael Berenbaum in J. Miller, *One, by One, by One* (Weidenfeld & Nicolson, 1990), pp. 222–3.
5. M. Geyer and M. Hanssen, 'German-Jewish Memory and National Consciouness' in Hartman (ed.), *Holocaust Remembrance*, pp. 175–90, p. 176.
6. A. Wieviorka, 'Testimony' in Hartman (ed.), *Holocaust Remembrance*, pp. 23–32, p. 32.
7. Berenbaum, *After Tragedy and Triumph* (CUP, 1990), p. 23.
8. A. Lerman, 'The Art of Holocaust Remembering' (*Jewish Quarterly* 1989, 135), pp. 24–32, p. 32.
9. E. Wiesel, 'Trivializing Memory' in *From the Kingdom of Memory* (NY: Summit Books, 1990), pp. 165–72, p. 168.
10. E. Wiesel, 'Foreword' in A. Insdorf, *Indelible Shadows: Film and the Holocaust*, Second Edition (CUP, 1989), pp. xi–xii, p. xii.

11. Alain Resnais, in Insdorf, *Indelible Shadows*, p. xix.
12. For a negative appraisal of *Night and Fog*, see M. Zyl and S. S. Friedman, 'The Holocaust as Seen in the Movies' in Friedman (ed.), *Holocaust Literature: A Handbook of Critical, Historical, and Literary Writings* (Westport: Greenwood Press, 1993), pp. 604–22, p. 618. For a positive assessment of the film, see I. Avisar, *Screening the Holocaust: Cinema's Images of the Unimaginable* (Bloomington: Indiana University Press, 1988), pp. 6–18.
13. Wiesel, 'Foreword', pp. xi–xii.
14. Wiesel, 'Trivializing Memory', p. 170.
15. Wiesel, 'Foreword', p. xii.
16. Wiesel, 'Foreword', p. xii.
17. Wiesel, 'Foreword', p. xi.
18. A. Rosenfeld, *A Double Dying: Reflections on Holocaust Literature* (Bloomington: Indiana University Press, 1980), pp. 82–114.
19. Rosenfeld, *A Double Dying*, p. 161.
20. Rosenfeld, *A Double Dying*, p. 173.
21. Peter Weiss, cited in Rosenfeld, *A Double Dying*, p. 158.
22. Rosenfeld, *A Double Dying*, p. 158. Rosenfeld's criticisms are echoed by Avisar, *Screening the Holocaust*, p. 91. For a slightly less critical view of Weiss, see J. E. Young, *Writing and Rewriting the Holocaust* (Bloomington: Indiana University Press, 1988), pp. 64–80.
23. W. Styron, *Sophie's Choice* (Corgi, 1980), p. 293.
24. Rosenfeld, *A Double Dying*, p. 160. Rosenfeld's criticisms are again echoed by Avisar in his reference to 'the obscenity of *Sophie's Choice* – as both a novel and a film' (*Screening the Holocaust*, p. 128).
25. Styron, in G. Telpaz, 'An Interview with William Styron' (*Partisan Review* 1985, 52:3), pp. 252–63, p. 256.
26. 'Lady Lazarus' in S. Plath, *Ariel* (Faber & Faber, 1965).
27. Rosenfeld, *A Double Dying*, p. 181. For a more sympathetic analysis of Plath's use of Holocaust imagery, see Young, *Writing and Rewriting the Holocaust*, pp. 117–33.
28. J. Doneson, *The Holocaust in American Film* (Philadelphia: JPSA, 1987), p. 8.
29. Young, *Writing and Rewriting the Holocaust*, p. 133.
30. John Simon, in Rosenfeld, *A Double Dying*, p. 118.
31. Styron, in Telpaz, 'An Interview with William Styron', p. 253.
32. Rosenfeld, *A Double Dying*, p. 29.
33. Styron, in Telpaz, 'An Interview with William Styron', p. 254.
34. C. Lanzmann, 'From the Holocaust to *Holocaust*' (*Dissent* 1981, 28:2), pp. 188–94, p. 190.
35. Wiesel, cited in Doneson, *The Holocaust in American Film*, p. 189.

36. Cited in Doneson, *The Holocaust in American Film*, p. 190.

37. S. Zielinski, 'History as Entertainment and Provocation' in A. Rabinbach and J. Zipes (eds.), *Germans and Jews since the Holocaust* (New York: Holmes & Meier, 1986), pp. 258–78, p. 73. For a more detailed discussion of the reception of *Holocaust* in West Germany, see pp. 185–283 of the same volume. For a more detailed discussion of the series' reception in the United States, see Doneson, *The Holocaust in American Film*, pp. 143–96.

38. C. James, 'Last Will and Testament', (*New Yorker* 23.5.88), pp. 86–92, p. 91.

39. E. Wiesel, 'Pilgrimage to the Kingdom of Night' in *From the Kingdom of Memory*, pp. 105–21, p. 114. It should be noted that, in its original context, Wiesel's comment refers to the Auschwitz State Museum.

40. Doneson, *The Holocaust in American Film*, p. 182.

41. L. Langer, 'The Americanization of the Holocaust on American Stage and Screen' in Langer, *Admitting the Holocaust: Collected Essays* (OUP, 1995), pp. 157–77, p. 175.

42. Avisar, *Screening the Holocaust*, p. 129; J. Berger, 'The Peril of Vulgarization' (*Dimensions* 1989, 5:1), pp. 3–6, p. 4.

43. Doneson, *The Holocaust in American Film*, p. 187.

44. *Jewish Chronicle* 2.9.94.

45. T. Rafferty, 'A Man of Transactions' (*New Yorker* 20.12.93), pp. 129–32, p. 132.

46. B. Cheyette, 'The Holocaust in the Picture-House' (*Times Literary Supplement* 18.2.94), pp. 18–19, p. 19.

47. A. Gross, letter (*Times Literary Supplement 18.3.94*).

48. W. Scammell, letter (*Times Literary Supplement 1.4.94*).

49. It should be noted that this scene has been praised by others. For example, Terrence Rafferty describes it as 'the most terrifying sequence ever filmed' ('A Man of Transactions', p. 132).

50. Simon Louvish, 'Witness' (*Sight and Sound* 1994, 4:3), pp. 12–15, p. 15. Such comments are echoed by Langer: 'Despite its candid representation of the ordeal of the Jews during World War II, even a blunt film like *Schindler's List* decides to leave us with memories of a healing wound rather than a throbbing scar.' (Introduction', *Admitting the Holocaust*, pp. 3–12, p. 11.)

51. Spielberg, in *Jewish Chronicle* 2.9.94.

52. Gross, letter.

53. All quotations are from C. Lanzmann, 'Twisted Truth of *Schindler's List*' (*Evening Standard* 10.2.94).

54. M. Ophuls, 'Closely Watched Trains' (*American Film* November 1985), pp. 16–27, p. 18, p. 79.

55. S. Ellicott, 'Lest We Forget' (*Sunday Times* 27.3.94).

56. In A. Hall, 'Shrine to Holocaust Victims' (*Daily Mirror* 29.8.94). It should also be noted that the success of the film had a further by-product: renewed interest in Thomas Keneally's book (upon which the film was based). As a result of the success of the film, the book was the second-best-selling paperback in the U.K. in 1994 (see *The Guardian* 10.1.95).
57. Spielberg, in Wapshott, 'The Return of the Prodigal', p. 9.
58. Spielberg, in J. Blair, 'Spielberg Comes of Age' (*Esquire* March 1994), pp. 62–66, p. 66.
59. Young, *Writing and Rewriting the Holocaust*, p. 44.

5

THE HOLOCAUST
AND JEWISH IDENTITY

Alongside concern over the use of the Holocaust in popular culture, general unease is now expressed over the increasing prominence granted to the subject in relation to the continuum of Jewish history and belief. No one is disputing the need to remember those who died, or to continue to pursue research in this area. What is questioned, however, is the increasing role played by the Holocaust in contemporary Jewish self-understanding. The former Chief Rabbi, Lord Jakobovits, was sufficiently concerned to issue a warning against 'the sanctification of the Holocaust as a cardinal doctrine of contemporary Jewish thought and practice'.[1] In a similar vein, the historian David Vital suggests that interest in the Holocaust supersedes interest in 'virtually all other developments, facets, and questions of Jewish life, history, and culture'.[2] A second historian, Evyatar Freisel, warns that 'a whole generation of young Jews has been educated about how the Jewish people died, but learnt very little about Jewish life – Jewish history, Jewish culture, Jewish beliefs.'[3] One consequence of this preoccupation is that, whereas there is an ever-growing number of Holocaust-related institutions and projects, it is often less easy to obtain financial support for Jewish studies *per se*.

Concern over the centrality of the Holocaust can take a number of forms: cultural, educational, political and religious. In the previous chapter, some of the concerns raised by the role of the Holocaust in popular culture were considered. In this chapter, the focus is on the question of what role – if any – the Holocaust should play in the formulation of Jewish identity. This question will be discussed primarily with reference to traditional responses, and to 'Holocaust theology'.

—— Traditional Responses to the Holocaust ——

Jews find in the Holocaust no new definition of Jewish identity because we need none. Nothing has changed. The tradition endures.[4]

With these words, Jacob Neusner encapsulates the traditional response to the Holocaust. The basic premise underlying such a response is that there is no unique challenge posed to faith. The Holocaust is seen as one in a long chain of catastrophes punctuating Jewish history; a list that includes the destruction of the Jerusalem Temple in 586 BCE and 70 CE; the Crusader massacres in 1096; the expulsion from Spain in 1492; the Chmielnicki massacres of 1648; and the pogroms in the Ukraine in 1881 and 1903. The biblical book of Lamentations was composed in response to the destruction of the Jerusalem Temple in 586 BCE. This text is read every year in synagogue on the 9 Av, the day in the liturgical calendar dedicated to remembrance of the destruction of the First and Second Temples. Alongside the text of Lamentations, *kinot* (dirges) are also read.[5] These *kinot* are modelled upon the biblical text and commemorate the victims of subsequent disasters. The destruction of the Jerusalem Temple thus serves as an archetype for all subsequent experiences of catastrophe. In this way, 'discrete historical catastrophes are drained of their discreteness and absorbed into a larger tradition.'[6] The victims of the Holocaust are to be remembered, but in the same manner as were the victims of previous disasters.

The belief that there is nothing theologically unique in the challenge posed by the Holocaust can be reflected in the terminology employed. For example, Jonathan Sacks and Eliezer Berkovits both prefer to speak of the holocaust with a lower-case 'h', thus indicating their belief that it is one in a series of similar events. Others prefer to speak of the (third) *Hurban* – a term traditionally applied to the destruction of the First and Second Temples. The use of either 'holocaust' or '*Hurban*' can serve to locate the event within the continuum of Jewish history and belief.

For a number of traditional thinkers, the Holocaust is not only the latest in a series of catastrophes to afflict the Jewish people, it is the problem of evil writ large. Berkovits argues that the theological problem is the same, regardless of whether it is the individual or the collective that suffers: 'The suffering of a single innocent child poses no less a problem to faith than the undeserved suffering of millions. As far as one's faith in a personal God is concerned, there is no difference between six, five, four million or one million.'[7] For both Berkovits and Sacks, the most convincing theological response to innocent suffering is that which interprets it as a consequence of the abuse of human freedom. In *Faith after the Holocaust*, Berkovits speaks of the hiding of God's face, *hester panim* (Isa. 45.15). God hides his face in order to enable humanity to exercise free will. However, if this exercise is to be meaningful, God cannot then intervene to prevent the consequences of the abuse of free will, even if this results in innocent suffering. Unfortunately, this non-intervention may well be experienced by the victim as divine indifference, for 'while God tolerates the sinner, he must abandon the victim; while he shows forbearance for the wicked, he must turn a deaf ear to the cries of the violated.'[8] Berkovits concludes that although the Holocaust was an absolute injustice, God could not intervene to prevent it without compromising human freedom. However, he insists that such a response is not indicative of 'a willingness to forgive the unheard cries of millions', but rather reflects 'a trust that in God the tragedy of man may find its transformation'.[9] For Berkovits, the establishment of the State of Israel in 1948, and the retaking of the Old City of Jerusalem in 1967, suggest that such trust is not misplaced.[10]

A second, but not necessarily incompatible, response is also in evidence. The appropriate response to suffering is not to speculate as to why it happened, but rather lies in a practical commitment to restore or rebuild that which has been broken. In the words of Rabbi Joseph Soloveitchik: 'We do not inquire about the hidden ways of the Almighty but, rather, about the path wherein man shall walk when suffering strikes. We ask neither about the cause of evil nor about its purpose but rather about how it might be mended and elevated.'[11] If this line of thinking is pursued, then the most traditional reactions of all are those found in the halakhic responses to the Holocaust.[12] It is estimated that at least half of the six million who died observed halakhah (Jewish law). If this was indeed the case, then the halakhic 'responsa' provide 'a unique record of Jewish religious life under the impact of the Holocaust'.[13] These responsa take the form of questions and answers (she'elot u-teshuvot) on particular points of halakhah. The rabbi would be asked to provide rulings on a variety of issues, ranging from queries about the observance of the food laws or festivals, to requests for advice as to the circumstances in which it was necessary to accept death for the sanctification of the Divine Name (kiddush hashem) rather than transgress halakhah.[14] The responsa are primarily concerned with practicalities. Rarely, if ever, do they speculate as to why such events should occur. This emphasis upon the practical, rather than the speculative, is also apparent in post-Holocaust Orthodox responses. Immanuel Jakobovits suggests that the most appropriate response to the Holocaust takes the form of a commitment to perpetuating both Judaism and Jewish life. What response could be more appropriate than 'to rebuild what has been destroyed and to ensure the continuity of Jewish life through the blessing of children and perpetuating their heritage'?[15]

On the rare occasions that halakhic responses do reflect upon possible reasons for suffering on such a scale, they generally conclude that it is a punishment for sin. Such a response is deeply traditional, building upon the schema laid out in Deuteronomy, and in the Blessings and Curses in particular (Deut. 27—30).[16] Underpinning such texts is the assumption that the basic paradigm of meaning is to be found in the covenantal relationship between God and Israel. This relationship is acted out in history, and therefore historical events serve as a commentary on the covenantal relationship, as 'barometers of God's disposition towards His people'.[17] Thus, according to Deuteronomy, prosperity and good fortune reflect God's blessing upon covenantal faithfulness (Deut. 28.1–2), whereas ill fortune and disaster are interpreted as the consequences of faithlessness (Deut. 28.15). Interpreting the Holocaust as a punishment for sin is one logical consequence of reading subsequent history in the light of this schema.

One thinker who interpreted the Holocaust along these lines was Rabbi Elchonon Wassermann of Baranowitch (1875–1941).[18] He developed his views in a treatise, In the Footsteps of the Messiah (Ikovossoh Demeshicho), written while he was travelling in the United States in 1938–9. Both Kristallnacht and the outbreak of war took place during the time of writing. Wassermann himself was shot by Latvian auxiliaries in Kovno on 6 July 1941. Wasserman interpreted the suffering of the Jews under the Nazis as evidence of 'the birth-pangs of the Messiah', the period between exile and redemption, 'a time of trouble, such as never has been' (Dan. 12.1). The Nazis were the agents of God's wrath, just as Nebuchadnezzar had been centuries previously (2 Chron. 36.17). For Wasserman, the sins for which the Jews were punished were those of assimilation, nationalism (Zionism), socialism and the denigration of Torah scholarship. Torah had been abandoned for the more secular attractions of assimilation into gentile society, or nationalism. He was adamant that the nature of the punishment indicated its cause. Jews were being expelled from the very societies to which they sought to gain admission: 'In Heaven two idolatries were fashioned into one – national-socialism. A terrible rod of fury was forged from them that strikes at Jews in every corner of the earth. The same abominations that we worshipped are now hammering us.'[19] Yet Wassermann remained convinced that the aim was not to destroy the Jewish people, but rather to call them to repentance and a return to Torah (Deut. 26.7; Isa. 59.20). In such a context, the suffering of the righteous sanctifies the Divine Name and atones for the sins of others. It is entirely consistent that Wassermann should interpret his own death in such terms:

> As we do Teshuvah we should [be concerned] with saving [the souls of] our American brothers and sisters, so they can continue as the Shearith Israel (the saving remnant). Let us go with raised heads. God

forbid, that any thought should enter anybody's mind which makes the sacrifice (*Korban*) unfit. We now carry out the greatest *Mitzvah*, *Kiddush Hashem* (sanctification of God's name). The fire which will burn our bodies, is the fire which will resurrect the Jewish people.[20]

Wassermann's views are echoed by others, such as Rabbi Yoel Teitelbaum of Satmar. By way of contrast, others such as Rabbi Immanuel Hartom accept the basic premise that the Holocaust was a punishment for sin, but differ in arguing that the sin concerned was *anti*-Zionism, rather than support for Zionism![21] Yet other Orthodox thinkers dissociate themselves from the suggestion that such suffering can be interpreted as a punishment for sin. Immanuel Jakobovits, for example, states that 'personally, together with countless others, I could not accept blaming any Jewish shortcomings as a specific cause of the Holocaust.'[22] While agreeing with such a viewpoint, Jonathan Sacks insists that it is essential to acknowledge that such arguments belong to 'a central tradition', and therefore cannot simply be dismissed.[23]

In spite of the diversity of viewpoints, traditional responses are nevertheless united by the conviction that the Holocaust poses no new challenge to faith. All remain convinced that 'the *meaning* of being a Jew has not changed with Auschwitz.'[24]

—— Holocaust Theology ——

The conviction that no new challenge is posed to faith is in stark contrast to the basic assumption of Holocaust theology. This assumption is best expressed by Richard Rubenstein, who in many ways provided the catalyst for the development of Holocaust theology when he published *After Auschwitz* in 1966: 'No Jewish theology will possess even a remote degree of relevance to contemporary Jewish life if it ignores the question of God and the death camps. That is *the question* for Jewish theology in our times.'[25] Rubenstein felt compelled to preface his book with such a claim because his thesis was that most attempts to formulate a Jewish theology since World War II 'seem to have been written as if the two decisive events of our time for Jews, the death camps and the birth of· Israel, had not taken place'.[26] The extent to which this situation has changed since the publication of *After Auschwitz* is apparent from the fact that there are now complaints that the Holocaust has assumed *too* prominent a place. Even those who disagree with the basic premise of Holocaust theology (such as Berkovits or Sacks) feel compelled to address the subject, if only to challenge the conclusions of Rubenstein and others.

While Rubenstein may well be the more radical thinker, it is Emil Fackenheim who has been described as 'the most influential thinker in religious and academic circles preoccupied with the Holocaust'.[27] A brief consideration of Fackenheim's position serves both to highlight the major preoccupations of Holocaust theology, and to indicate why such an approach disturbs more traditional thinkers. Given his current association with Holocaust theology, it is ironic that Fackenheim did not feel the need to address the subject until 1967. His earlier work fits the pattern described by Rubenstein in his preface to *After Auschwitz*: up until the mid–1960s, Fackenheim did not consider the death camps and the State of Israel to be issues of particular significance. The turning-point came when he reached the conclusion that 'at least *Jewish* faith is, after all, *not absolutely* immune to *all* empirical events.'[28] Previously, Fackenheim had started from the assumption that faith is, or should be, immune to the vicissitudes of human history. Given such a view, he originally regarded the Holocaust as nothing more, and nothing less, than an example of the problem of evil.

With this shift in perspective, Fackenheim came to see Jewish history as consisting of 'root experiences' and 'epoch-making events'. 'Root experiences' are those events that constitute the Jewish faith, namely the Exodus and the giving of the Law on Sinai. Such events bear witness to the commanding and saving presence of God. 'Epoch-making events' reflect key moments in the conflict between covenantal promise (symbolized by the root experiences) and historical counter-testimony. As examples of epoch-making events, Fackenheim lists the end of prophecy, the destruction of the First Temple, the Maccabean revolt, the destruction of the Second Temple, and the expulsion from Spain. These events do not create a new faith, but rather pose a fundamental challenge to the existing faith. The Holocaust is the supreme epoch-making event. As such, it threatens to shatter faith.

The problem for faith posed by the Holocaust has its roots in the realization that 'a Jew today is one who, except for an historical accident – Hitler's loss of the war – would have either been murdered or never been born.'[29] For Fackenheim, it is necessary to recognize that those Jews who are alive today are not 'a holy remnant', but rather 'an accidental remnant'.[30] To be meaningful, any articulation of Jewish identity must take this fact into account. His conclusion is that after the Holocaust this 'accidental remnant' is confronted by a dilemma:

> If a post-Holocaust Jew continues to bring up children, he is implicated in the possible murder of his children, for what was once possible is possible ever after. And if, refusing to be implicated in

murder, he has no children, he does his share in making an end to both Jews and Judaism. Collectively, then, the post-Holocaust Jew is either a potential murderer or a suicide: either way Hitler wins.[31]

The only way out of this dilemma lies with an additional, 614th commandment that has its origins in Auschwitz. In Rubenstein's opinion, 'no passage by a contemporary Jewish religious thinker has become as well known' as Fackenheim's formulation.[32] The 614th commandment takes the form of four imperatives, two positive and two negative:

> We are, first, commanded to survive as Jews, lest the Jewish people perish. We are commanded, second, to remember in our very guts and bones the martyrs of the Holocaust, lest their memory perish. We are forbidden, thirdly, to deny or despair of God, however much we may have to contend with Him, lest Judaism perish. We are forbidden, finally, to despair of the world as the place which is to become the kingdom of God, lest we help make it a meaningless place in which God is dead or irrelevant and everything is permitted. To abandon any of these imperatives, in response to Hitler's victories at Auschwitz, would be to hand him yet other, posthumous victories.[33]

The resonance that this formulation found within the wider community reflects its ability to provide an explanation both of what it means to be Jewish, and of what is distinctive about Jews as a group. By placing such emphasis on remembrance and the survival of the Jewish people, Fackenheim articulates a response to the Holocaust that purports to transcend the divide between secular and religious Jews. Anyone who is committed to Jewish survival is responding, either explicitly or implicitly, to the 614th commandment. Thus, 'a Jewish commitment to Jewish survival is a monumental act of faithfulness, as well as a monumental albeit as yet fragmentary, act of faith.'[34] Above all, such a commitment signifies a very real determination not to hand Hitler 'yet other, posthumous victories'.

In responding to criticism of the 614th commandment, Fackenheim developed his argument further. He acknowledges that it is not enough for Auschwitz to bear witness to the commanding presence of God. For faith to continue, there must also be some evidence of a divine saving presence. Fackenheim locates this saving presence in acts of armed and unarmed resistance. As examples of such resistance, he cites the Warsaw Ghetto fighters, Hasidim going singing to their deaths, and women continuing to give birth in the ghettos and death camps. He suggests that all such actions are a form of *tikkun* (repair or restoration). These acts are motivated by a commitment to the ongoing survival of the Jewish people and of Judaism. Such a commitment to survival arises in response to the Commanding Voice of Auschwitz. To support his argument, Fackenheim appeals to 'an historic statement' by Pelagia Lewinska, a Polish survivor of Auschwitz:

> They had condemned us to die in our own filth, to drown in our own excrement. They wished to abase us, to destroy our human dignity, to efface every vestige of humanity, to return us to the level of wild animals, to fill us with horror and contempt toward ourselves and our fellows.
>
> But from the instant that I grasped the motivating principle . . . it was as if I had been awakened from a dream. . . . I felt under orders to live. And if I did die in Auschwitz, it would be as a human being, I would hold on to my dignity. I was not going to become the contemptible, disgusting brute my enemy wished me to be.[35]

Lewinska's sense of being 'under orders to live' is, in Fackenheim's view, nothing less than a response to the 614th commandment. Such acts of resistance provide a bridge connecting the Holocaust to those who come after. Faith *after* the Holocaust is only possible because of the faith inherent in such acts of *tikkun* during the Holocaust.[36]

Fackenheim offers a coherent, clearly argued response to the Holocaust. It is a response that has met with a positive reception, particularly in the United States. He succeeds in articulating an understanding of Judaism that gives expression both to a commitment to Jewish survival, and to 'the communal emotions of amazement and awe in response to those who were able to resist'.[37] However, perhaps precisely because of this positive reception, Fackenheim's approach has been subject to considerable criticism, particularly from more Orthodox quarters.[38] Two primary objections tend to dominate. First, critics suggest that a commitment to Jewish survival and to remembering the victims of catastrophe has always been a part of Judaism. There is no need for an additional 614th commandment: it contains nothing that is not already present in the original 613. Jews should therefore respond to the Holocaust in the same way as they have responded to catastrophes in the past – by rebuilding their lives and attempting to restore what they can of that which has been lost.

Second, critics accuse Fackenheim of building a theology, and an understanding of Jewish identity, upon negative foundations. Jews are to survive as Jews for the simple reason that to do otherwise would be to hand Hitler 'yet other, posthumous victories'. Ironically, Hitler's determination to destroy the Jewish people becomes an intrinsic part of a contemporary formulation of Jewish identity: a Jew is anyone who would potentially have been a victim under the terms of the Nuremberg Laws. For Fackenheim's critics, such a definition of Jewish identity in itself hands Hitler a 'posthumous victory'. It builds Jewish self-understanding around a Nazi definition of Jewishness. For Jakobovits, Sacks et al., defining Jewishness in this way evacuates it of any meaningful, positive content. They argue that, if Jewish survival is to have any positive meaning, it must be built upon something more than resistance to Hitler. Sacks' critique of Fackenheim is typical. He praises him for attempting to rescue something positive from the Holocaust (a commitment to Jewish survival), but concludes:

> Fackenheim has erred in building a Jewish theology on the very foundations of the holocaust. That way, madness lies. There is no way of building Jewish existence on a command to spite Hitler. That is giving too much to Hitler and too little to God. The people Israel did not survive Egypt to spite Pharaoh, nor did it survive Purim so as not to hand Haman a posthumous victory.[39]

Are such criticisms valid? The answer to such a question ultimately depends on whether one accepts that the Holocaust poses a challenge to faith different to that of previous catastrophes. If it does not, then the traditional responses are as valid now as they were in the past. However, it is the contention of Fackenheim and others engaged in articulating Holocaust theology that this is no longer the case. He insists that we must accept that 'what was once possible is possible ever after'. By proposing the 614th commandment as a response to the Holocaust, Fackenheim is asserting that the situation in which Jews find themselves *has changed*. To carry on as if it has not is at best naive, and at worst irresponsible. Hence his insistence that the most appropriate response to the Holocaust takes the form of support for the State of Israel, the ultimate guarantor of Jewish survival.[40] In effect, Fackenheim is agreeing with the view that:

> After the Holocaust all those nice distinctions that Jews make in relation to their identities have precious little meaning: *all* kinds of Jews, regardless of their identities and even religions, found themselves in the gas chambers at Auschwitz – and that is the only fixed reality that Jews know or ought to know about themselves.[41]

If the Jews were 'a holy remnant', then such 'nice distinctions' concerning identity would be of primary significance. In Fackenheim's view, however, Jews are 'an accidental remnant'. As a consequence, identity as a community of fate is of primary importance, whereas internal differences over what it means to be Jewish are of secondary significance.

—— *Solidarity with the Jewish Fate* ——

Fackenheim's reflections on post-Holocaust existence as 'an accidental remnant', together with the worst fears of his critics, find their logical fulfilment in the work of a number of more secular writers. For such writers, 'the Nazi Holocaust is henceforth the absolute and radical reference point for the existence of every Jew.'[42] Two examples of this approach will suffice. The first (which will be considered in more detail) is the philosopher Jean Améry (1912–78). The second is the Polish journalist, Adam Michnik.

Améry was a survivor of Auschwitz. He committed suicide on 17 October 1978. In 1966 he published an essay, 'On the Impossibility and Necessity of Being a Jew',[43] an analysis of what it means to be 'an accidental remnant', particularly for those Jews with no religious affiliations. Améry reflects on the dilemma confronting those who, like himself, define themselves as a 'Catastrophe Jew', a 'Jew without positive determinants'.[44] For such individuals, Nazism and the Holocaust revealed the 'necessity' of being a Jew: Améry was a Jew simply because that was how he was defined under the Nuremberg Laws. As a consequence of this legal definition he was first tortured and then sent to Auschwitz. For Jews such as Améry, 'being Jewish burst upon them with elemental force', as something imposed from the outside rather than willingly embraced.[45] He recalls that reading of the Nuremberg Laws in a newspaper brought with it the realization that:

> Society, concretized in the National Socialist German state, which the world recognized absolutely as the legitimate representative of the German people, had just made me formally and beyond any question a Jew, or rather it had given a new dimension to what I had already known earlier, but which at the time was of no great consequence to me, namely, that I was a Jew.[46]

The essence of this Nazi definition was that a Jew was nothing more than 'a dead man on leave, someone to be murdered, who only by chance was not yet where he properly belonged'.[47] In Améry's view, such a definition of Jewishness 'reads more briefly than the Pentateuch or the Talmud and yet provides more precise information. It is more binding as a basic formula of Jewish existence.'[48]

The 'necessity' of being a Jew, as symbolized by the Nuremberg Laws, exists alongside an equally binding 'impossibility'. According to

Améry, 'one can re-establish the link with a tradition that one has lost, but one cannot freely invent it for oneself.'[49] He remained adamant that his own background contained no such 'link' with Jewish tradition. Prior to the rise of Nazism he had been a thoroughly assimilated Austrian, raised in a Catholic environment, who regarded German language and culture as 'home'. The Nuremberg Laws signified the irrevocable loss of this identity and the imposition, in its place, of another. This verdict had to be accepted because it reflected the determination of the German people to expel Jews from German history and culture.[50] As a statement of intent, the Nuremberg Laws asserted that German Jews were no longer – and indeed never had been – an authentic part of that history and culture. Such an abrupt loss of identity could not simply be replaced by the assumption of another, particularly one imposed by those who denied that individual's right to a previously assumed German identity. Thus, for Améry, the 'impossibility of being a Jew' is reflected in the fact that 'with Jews as Jews I share practically nothing: no language, no cultural tradition, no childhood memories.'[51] All that he did share with his fellow Jews was 'solidarity in the face of threats'.[52] His conclusion is that the only possible response to the 'necessity and impossibility of being a Jew' is to embrace the identity imposed from outside while clearly recognizing it for what it is: Jewishness 'without positive determinants'.

Améry's comments find an echo, twenty-five years later, in a speech by the Polish journalist, Adam Michnik. In this speech, Michnik expressed his reservations about being named 'Jew of the Year'. He reflects on his understanding of Jewish solidarity:

> I feel solidarity with something more than just the ashes of my murdered grandparents. I am not speaking of solidarity with Jewish history or with the Jewish religion, or Jewish traditions, or customs, or with the Jewish nation or the state of Israel. With what then? When I look for words to describe this complicated and intimate feeling, what comes to mind is solidarity with the Jewish fate. The Jewish fate is that of a threatened people who have suffered many blows, who know the taste of humiliation, of defeat, and who have always faced hard choices. It is finally the fate of a people who have been rejected and persecuted.[53]

Michnik's sense of 'solidarity with the Jewish fate' echoes Améry's understanding of the 'impossibility of being a Jew' other than as 'solidarity in the face of threats'. Both dissociate themselves from any 'positive' understanding of Jewish identity, such as a commitment to Judaism. They can therefore be seen to offer two illustrations of what

75

post-Holocaust existence as 'an accidental remnant' might mean. Michnik and Améry also fulfil the worst fears of more traditional thinkers: they reduce Jewish experience to a history of catastrophe, the story of 'a people who have been rejected and persecuted'. Does this understanding of a Jewish identity 'without positive determinants' represent a 'posthumous victory' for Hitler? Or is it a response to the fact that the Holocaust is now 'the absolute and radical reference point for the existence of every Jew'? In other words, is the only choice available that between the traditional denial of the uniqueness of the Holocaust on the one hand, and Améry and Michnik's proposal of an identity that consists solely of 'solidarity in the face of threats' on the other?

A third possibility lies in contemporary mythologization of the Holocaust as expressed in the emergence of a new 'Judaism of Holocaust and Redemption'. This understanding of Judaism emphasizes the uniqueness of the Holocaust, but also attempts to provide a sense of identity with positive determinants by balancing this with an emphasis upon redemption, particularly as symbolized by the State of Israel. The Judaism of Holocaust and Redemption will be the subject of the following chapter.

NOTES

1. I. Jakobovits, 'Some Personal, Theological and Religious Reflections on the Holocaust' (*Holocaust and Genocide Studies* 1988, 3:4), pp. 371–81, p. 371.
2. D. Vital, 'After the Catastrophe' in P. Hayes (ed.), *Lessons and Legacies* (Evanston: Northwestern University Press, 1991), pp. 120–38, pp. 136–7.
3. E. Freisel, 'The Holocaust in Jewish Consciousness' in J. Webber (ed.), *Jewish Identities in the New Europe* (Littman Library of Jewish Civilization, 1994), pp. 228–34, p. 230.
4. J. Neusner, 'The Implications of the Holocaust' (*Journal of Religion* 1973, 53:3), pp. 293–308, p. 308.
5. See A. Rosenfeld (ed.), *Kinot for the Ninth of Av* (New York: Judaica Press, 1965).
6. A. Mintz, *Hurban* (New York: Columbia Press, 1984), p. 103.
7. E. Berkovits, *Faith after the Holocaust* (New York: KTAV, 1973), p. 128.
8. Berkovits, *Faith after the Holocaust*, p. 106. Berkovits' views have parallels in the 'soul-making' theodicy of John Hick. See Hick's *Evil and the God of Love* (London: Macmillan, 1966, 1985).

9. Berkovits, *Faith after the Holocaust*, p. 136.

10. Berkovits, *Faith after the Holocaust*, pp. 144–69.

11. J. Soloveitchik, 'Kol Dodi Dofek: It is the Voice of My Beloved that Knocketh' in B. Rosenberg and F. Heuman (eds.), *Theological and Halakhic Reflections on the Holocaust* (New York: KTAV, 1992), pp. 51–117, p. 56.

12. For more on halakhic responses to the Holocaust, see Rosenberg and Heuman (eds.), *Theological and Halakhic Responses to the Holocaust*; R. Kirschner, *Rabbinic Responses of the Holocaust Era* (New York: Schocken Books, 1985); and I. Rosenbaum, *Holocaust and Halakhah* (New York: KTAV, 1976).

13. Kirschner, *Rabbinic Responses of the Holocaust Era*, p. 16.

14. For more detail on *kiddush hashem* in relation to the Holocaust, see Kirschner, *Rabbinic Responses of the Holocaust Era*, pp. 111–23; and Rosenbaum, *Holocaust and Halakhah*, pp. 17–59.

15. Jakobovits, 'Some Personal, Theological and Religious Responses to the Holocaust', p. 380.

16. Punishment for sin is not the only explanation of suffering to be found in the Hebrew Bible. Other responses include: suffering is a mystery or inexplicable (Job 36.26, 38); evil is a human characteristic (Gen. 6.5; Jer. 3.17); God creates both good and evil (Isa. 45.6; Job 1—2); suffering is unjust and either reflects God's hiding of his face (Isa. 45.15, Ps. 44.23–6), or inspires the sufferer to proclaim his innocence and demand a response from God (Job).

17. A. Berger, *Crisis and Covenant* (Albany: State University of New York Press, 1985), p. 1.

18. For more detail on Wassermann, see G. Greenberg, 'Orthodox Theological Responses to *Kristallnacht*' (*Holocaust and Genocide Studies* 1988, 3:4), pp. 431–42.

19. Wassermann, cited in Menachem Friedman, 'The Haredim and the Holocaust' (*Jerusalem Quarterly*, Winter 1990, 53), pp. 86–114.

20. Wassermann, cited in Greenberg, 'Orthodox Theological Responses to *Kristallnacht*', p. 439.

21. J. Sacks, *Tradition in an Untraditional Age* (Vallentine Mitchell, 1990), pp. 142–4.

22. Jakobovits, 'Some Personal, Theological and Religious Responses to the Holocaust', p. 377.

23. Sacks, *Tradition in an Untraditional Age*, p. 142.

24. Jakobovits, 'Some Personal, Theological and Religious Responses to the Holocaust', p. 372.

25. R. L. Rubenstein, *After Auschwitz* (Bloomington: Bobbs-Merrill, 1966), p. x.

26. R. L. Rubenstein, 'Preface to the First Edition', in *After Auschwitz*, Second Edition (Baltimore: John Hopkins University Press, 1992).

27. R. Alter, 'Deformations of the Holocaust' (*Commentary* February 1981), pp. 48–54, p. 52. For more detail on Fackenheim's response to the Holocaust, see: *God's Presence in History* (New York: New York University Press, 1970); *The Jewish Return into History* (New York: Schocken Books, 1978); *To Mend the World* (New York: Schocken Books, 1982).

28. Fackenheim, *To Mend the World*, p. 13.

29. Fackenheim, *To Mend the World*, p. 295.

30. Fackenheim, *To Mend the World*, p. 308.

31. E. L. Fackenheim, 'The Development of My Thought', (*Religious Studies Review* 1987, 13:3), pp. 204–6, p. 205.

32. Rubenstein, *After Auschwitz*, Second Edition, p. 180.

33. E. L. Fackenheim, 'Jewish Values in the Post-Holocaust Future' (*Judaism* 1967, 16:3), pp. 266–99, p. 272.

34. Fackenheim, *The Jewish Return into History*, p. 31.

35. Cited in Fackenheim, *To Mend the World*, p. 217.

36. Fackenheim, *To Mend the World*, pp. 201–313.

37. M. Oppenheim, 'Theology and Community' (*Religious Studies Review* 1987, 13:3), pp. 206–10, p. 207.

38. For a sample of the criticism levelled at Fackenheim's position, see: Sacks, *Tradition in an Untraditional Age*, pp. 149–51; S. Cain, 'Questions and Answers after Auschwitz' (*Judaism* 1971, 20:3), pp. 263–78; S. T. Katz, *Post-Holocaust Dialogues* (New York: New York University Press, 1983), pp. 205–47; M. Meyer, 'Judaism after Auschwitz' (*Commentary* June 1972, 53), pp. 55–62; M. Wyschogrod, 'Faith after the Holocaust' (*Judaism* 1971, 20:3), pp. 286–94.

39. Sacks, *Tradition in an Untraditional Age*, p. 151.

40. Fackenheim, *The Jewish Return into History*, pp. 43–57, pp. 273–86.

41. J. Webber, 'Modern Jewish Identities', in *Jewish Identities in the New Europe*, pp. 74–85, p. 85.

42. Cited in Jean Améry, *At the Mind's Limits* (New York: Schocken Books, 1986), p. 92.

43. In Améry, *At the Mind's Limits*, pp. 82–101.

44. Améry, *At the Mind's Limits*, p. 94.

45. Améry, *At the Mind's Limits*, p. 94.

46. Améry, *At the Mind's Limits*, p. 85.

47. Améry, *At the Mind's Limits*, p. 86.

48. Améry, *At the Mind's Limits*, p. 94.

49. Améry, *At the Mind's Limits*, p. 84.

50. For a more detailed discussion of this theme, see Améry's essay, 'How Much Home Does a Person Need?' in *At the Mind's Limits*, pp. 41–61.

51. Améry, *At the Mind's Limits*, p. 97.

52. Améry, *At the Mind's Limits*, p. 98.

53. A. Michnik, 'Poland and the Jews' (*New York Review of Books* 30.5.91), pp. 11–12, p. 12.

6

THE MYTHOLOGIZATION
OF THE HOLOCAUST

The *myth* of the Holocaust now takes the place of the Holocaust itself.[1]

Today there is widespread unease concerning 'the cultural, political and religious uses' to which the Holocaust has been put.[2] In Orthodox circles, there is concern that ethnicity and/or a commitment to the rhetoric of remembrance is emerging as an alternative to traditional definitions of Jewish identity (as, for example, in the theology of Emil Fackenheim). Other critics, such as Marc Ellis and Amos Oz, suggest that continuing preoccupation with the Holocaust and victimization serves to prevent the normalization of relations between the State of Israel and the non-Jewish world. They argue that the Holocaust has been, and continues to be, 'misused' for political purposes. Despite very different agendas, these critics are united by a concern that contemporary Jewish preoccupation with the Holocaust is taking the form of a 'mythologization' of these events.

Four beliefs, although rarely fully articulated, underpin popular perceptions of the Holocaust. The first affirms the centrality of remembrance as a sacred duty, a debt to the dead. The second asserts that the Holocaust is unique, and demands that a qualitative distinction be drawn between the fate of the Jews and the suffering of other victims of the Nazis. Third is the claim that the Holocaust is ineffable: its scale is such that the experience cannot be fully communicated or represented – even by those who were there. Finally, there is the conviction that having happened once the Holocaust could happen again; hence the need for constant vigilance (expressed through commitment to education, support for the State of Israel, opposition to antisemitism and racism, and so on). That there are implicit contradictions between some of these beliefs is rarely, if ever, acknowledged. Yet the very existence of such contradictions serves to generate much of the contemporary debate concerning appropriate forms of remembrance. As Charles Maier notes, 'Jewish suffering is depicted as ineffable, uncommunicable, and yet always to be proclaimed. It is intensely private, not to be diluted, but simultaneously public so that gentile society will confirm the crimes.'[3]

Contradictory or otherwise, these beliefs nevertheless constitute a recognizable rhetoric of remembrance. Such rhetoric is often expressed in shorthand, as in the use of the slogans 'Zakhor!' ('Remember') and 'Never again'. Likewise, Auschwitz frequently serves to represent the experience of the Holocaust as a whole. The increasingly widespread use of this sort of rhetoric is indicative of the emergence of the Holocaust as a modern myth. Given the popular understanding of myth as something unbelievable or false, it is important to stress that the term is being used here in its technical anthropological sense to refer to 'a story which evokes strong emotions and transmits and reinforces back societal values'.[4] Communicated through narrative and ritual, myths serve to express a community's sense of its position in relation to the world: 'the myths that groups tell about themselves express the perception that the group has of its past, the way it remembers the past, and the significance it attributes to the past.'[5] Understood in mythological terms, the Holocaust becomes 'a transcendent event which precedes and qualifies any attempt to fashion a modern Jewish identity'.[6]

As early as 1986, Claude Lanzmann suggested that public discussion about the Holocaust had taken on 'all the characteristics of a mythical account; as knowledge of the unknowable, it is blurred, vague and stereotyped.'[7] Both the widespread usage of a generalized term such as 'Holocaust' to represent these events, and the emergence of Auschwitz as a symbol for the whole, serve to illustrate this process. While Auschwitz is widely remembered, other killing centres (such as Belzec and Chelmno) are largely forgotten. One consequence of this preoccupation with Auschwitz is that the memory of the death camps often comes to dominate or subsume that of other aspects of the Holocaust, such as the ghettos or the activities of the *Einsatzgruppen*. The significance of the geography, chronological development and contemporary reality of the camp is minimized or overlooked. During the course of the Carmelite controversy it became apparent that there is little or no place for the Polish experience of Auschwitz in popular Jewish perceptions of the Holocaust. The mythological character of contemporary remembrance of the Holocaust finds typical expression in continued reliance on the threefold categories of victim, bystander and perpetrator. The use of such categories invites the drawing of absolute distinctions between the experiences of particular groups, such as Jews and Poles. In this schema, if the Jews are victims, then the Poles must be, by definition, either bystanders or perpetrators – a reading of history that is, unsurprisingly, considered offensive by many Poles. The tendency to render absolute the distinction between the experiences of various groups in turn leads to the creation of taboos. The existence of such taboos is evident from the inordinate amount of attention paid to the question of who has the 'right' to speak and what can legitimately be said. Debates over what constitutes an 'authentic' or 'inauthentic' response to the Holocaust recur whenever some boundary (whether of taste or propriety) is perceived to have been crossed. In such a context, the Carmelite controversy can be interpreted as a conflict between Jewish and Polish mythological perceptions of Auschwitz.

Jacob Neusner goes further and suggests that alongside this general process of mythologization, we can also chart the emergence of a 'Judaism of Holocaust and Redemption'.[8] He claims that, in conjunction with the State of Israel, the Holocaust has come to provide a mythic framework circumscribing many Jews' perception of what it means to be Jewish, both on its own terms and in relation to the world. Neusner's analysis provides a variation upon Fackenheim's understanding of post-Holocaust Jewish identity as an 'accidental remnant'. By linking the Holocaust to the State of Israel, the Judaism of Holocaust and Redemption offers a mythic framework that purports to 'make sense' of Jewish existence since 1945.

—— *The Judaism of Holocaust and* ——
Redemption

Linking the Holocaust to the State of Israel generates a redemptive myth of death to rebirth:

> The Judaism of Holocaust and Redemption . . . takes as its ineluctable question the meaning of Jewish existence after the systematic murder of most of the Jews of Europe and offers as its self-evident reply the proposition that the redemption constituted by the creation of the State of Israel serves as the other half of the whole story of the meaning of what has happened.[9]

This mythic framework echoes the classical biblical paradigm of catastrophe and redemption, expressed in the Deuteronomic Curses and Blessings and the sequence of destruction-exile-restoration. Michael Berenbaum suggests that such a mythic linkage is understandable, perhaps even inevitable, for 'in a sense, the Holocaust can only be accepted religiously as a prelude to redemption.'[10] Neusner himself attaches great significance to the fact that this myth of catastrophe and redemption only assumed fully fledged form *after* the Six Day War: it is the events of the summer of 1967, rather than the establishment of the State of Israel in 1948, which provide the true mythic counterpart to the Holocaust: 'the extermination of European Jewry could become *the* Holocaust only on 9 July when in the aftermath of a remarkable victory, the State of Israel celebrated the return of the people of Israel to the ancient wall of the Temple in Jerusalem.'[11] Given the supercharged atmosphere of the days preceding the war (with fears of a 'second Holocaust' widespread), it was perhaps inevitable that the dramatic successes of the Israeli Defence Forces should take on messianic overtones.[12] In mythic terms, whilst the Holocaust bore witness to the destruction of an estimated one third of world Jewry, the events of 1948 and 1967 combined in symbolizing the end of exile and the restoration of Jewish sovereignty.

The appeal of such a system is evident. First, it offers a clear and, on its own terms, unambiguous answer to the question: 'why be Jewish?' The 'answer' provided by the Holocaust is that there is no choice. In effect, the Judaism of Holocaust and Redemption synthesizes Fackenheim's 'accidental remnant' with Améry's 'Catastrophe Jew': Jewish identity is presented as inescapable fact. Second, this mythic framework, with its attendant definition of Jewishness, inhabits the middle ground between 'a genuinely religious and an entirely secular system'.[13] It therefore provides a bridge between a purely secular understanding of Jewish identity on the one hand, and a more strictly Orthodox definition on the other. For example, activities such as fundraising and visiting Israel or the sites of destruction in Europe, which on the surface seem to be non-religious, take on heightened significance. As a result, the myth of Holocaust and Redemption serves to provide the necessary framework for Jewish civil religion in Israel and the United States.

—— Jewish Civil Religion ——

Civil religion embodies characteristics of traditional religion – it projects a meaning system, expressed with symbols – but at its core stands a corporate identity rather than a transcendent power, even if it also refers to transcendent reality or even a supernatural power.[14]

Jewish civil religion builds upon the assumption that 'the feeling of interdependence, of a common fate, represents the widest minimal basis, the common denominator, of Jewish belonging in our times.'[15] As a consequence, the Jewish people and their 'return into history' become the focus of attention. The Holocaust and the establishment of the State of Israel provide two poles circumscribing contemporary Jewish existence. The Holocaust offers the most radical demonstration to date of 'the unity in fate of the Jewish people' and serves to highlight the precarious nature of Jewish existence, particularly in the Diaspora.[16] That it was followed within three years by the creation of the State of Israel serves as evidence of the tenacity of Jewish survival in the face of threat. Within Israeli civil religion, each of these events has its attendant symbols and rituals, including Yad Vashem and Yom Hashoah in the case of the Holocaust, and the Western Wall, the national anthem and flag, and Yom Haatzmaut (Independence Day) in the case of the establishment of the State of Israel.[17]

By framing these two events as a myth of catastrophe and redemption, Jewish civil religion embodies an interpretation of history in which the Jewish people are 'a people dwelling alone' (Num. 23.9) surrounded by real or potential enemies, constantly threatened with extinction, yet nevertheless continuing to survive against the odds. Simon Rawidowicz summarizes this approach: 'There is no nation more dying than Israel, yet none better equipped to resist disaster, to fight alone, always alone.'[18] In such a context, the State of Israel is presented as the Jewish people's response to the Holocaust. The State itself is conceived of as both a fitting memorial to those who died, and as the only reliable guarantee against any potential repetition: it is the embodiment of the Jewish people's commitment to 'never again'. Such an understanding constantly surfaces in the rhetoric of Israel's political leaders, particularly at the time of Yom Hashoah. Typical is a comment by Moshe Dayan: 'The historical heritage of the six million — the historical imperative they left us — is to make sure that such a thing won't happen again.'[19] More recently, on visiting Auschwitz in April 1992, Lieutenant General Ehud Barak, Chief of the Israeli General Staff, stated that 'the Israeli Defence Forces symbolize for the State of Israel our promise and sworn oath that what happened here will never happen again.'[20]

For Jacob Neusner, this myth of Judaism and Redemption in its Israeli form serves a clear functional purpose:

> The place of the Holocaust in the civil religion of the State of Israel is easy to understand: it forms a critical element in the public explanation of why there must be a State of Israel, why it must be of its present character and not some other, and why every citizen must be prepared to support the State in peacetime and fight for it in war.[21]

However, he is less than convinced of its relevance for Jews living in the United States. He dismisses the American Judaism of Holocaust and Redemption as a vehicle of ethnic self-assertion for American Jews: 'It is what sets them apart from the others while giving them a claim upon those others.'[22] As a consequence, Neusner interprets the opening of the USHMM as marking the triumphant climax of the American Judaism of Holocaust and Redemption. The fact that the Museum was built on federal land in the heart of the nation's capital, and opened by President Clinton, stands as testimony to the American Jewish community's success in introducing the memory of the Holocaust into the heart of the civic culture of the United States. However, far from agreeing with this interpretation of the opening of the USHMM as a triumphant success, Neusner sees it as proof of an obsession that ultimately threatens the future of American Judaism. His criticisms echo those of the Orthodox thinkers considered in the previous chapter. He argues that to build an understanding of Jewish identity upon the Holocaust is ultimately self-defeating: 'The opening ceremony for the Holocaust museum reached its climax in the recital of Kaddish. Some wonder whether the angels above were not weeping for that other-worldly religion, Judaism, which, for American Jews, is now mostly a faded memory.'[23] In view of such comments, it comes as little surprise to find that the Chief Rabbi, Jonathan Sacks, wholeheartedly endorses Neusner's critique of the American Judaism of Holocaust and Redemption as reductionist: 'The civil religion of American Jews is not Judaism. It focuses on public occasions rather than private life. Its forum is not the synagogue but fund-raising dinners, missions to Israel, and the aspects and occasions of secular Jewish organizational life.'[24]

Neusner, however, differs slightly in emphasis from Sacks. While agreeing that 'Jews find in the Holocaust no new definition of Jewish identity for we need none', he is less dismissive of the value of civil Judaism per se.[25] Whereas Sacks appears to object to any non-Orthodox definition of Jewish identity, Neusner seems happy to acknowledge the value of a myth of Holocaust and Redemption as the basis for Israeli civil religion. What he appears to object to is the application of this myth to a North American context. For Neusner the Judaism of Holocaust and Redemption is inappropriate, even illegitimate, in the context of the United States for the simple reason that American Jews have chosen not to live in Israel. If, mythically understood, the State of Israel constitutes the Jewish people's response to the Holocaust, how can American Jews subscribe to this myth yet persist in living outside Israel? His view is that subscribing to this myth has seriously dysfunctional consequences for American Jews: it serves to distance them from the reality of which they have chosen to be a part. In effect, Neusner accuses American Jews of employing the myth of Holocaust and Redemption to construct an identity alien to the circumstances in which they live.

Jonathan Woocher is considerably less critical in his evaluation of American civil Judaism. He suggests that if there is a weakness in the American version of the myth of Holocaust and Redemption, it lies in the tendency of American Jews to create an idealized, romanticized image of the State of Israel precisely because of their distance from the reality. Rather than being dysfunctional, Woocher argues that the American Judaism of Holocaust and Redemption is profoundly functional: it serves to articulate an understanding of Judaism as 'an activist religion emphasizing the pursuit of Jewish unity and distinctiveness on the one hand and the rootedness of American Jews in American society on the other'.[26] Thus, while sharing a belief in the providential and redemptive character of the State of Israel, the American version of the myth stresses the importance of the support (financial, moral and political) provided by Jews *outside* of Israel. Stress is laid upon the mutual responsibility and interdependence of the State of Israel and Jews in the Diaspora (and in particular, in the United States). According to Michael Berenbaum, the establishment of the USHMM in Washington DC can be interpreted as a statement of intent, a declaration by the American Jewish community that it has come of age as a partner, rather than a dependent, of the State of Israel. As such, it is entitled to articulate its own memory and understanding of the Holocaust. It is this memory that is embodied in the USHMM and memorials and museums throughout the country.[27]

—— *A Surplus of Memory?* ——

Whereas the disagreement between Woocher and Neusner is over the applicability of a myth of Holocaust and Redemption to the United States, others question the helpfulness of any such mythological interpretation of these events. Such criticism takes two very different forms. The first suggests that, alongside the continuing imperative to remember the Holocaust, there is also a pressing need to forget. The second argues that the mythologization of the Holocaust is itself a form of forgetfulness – amnesia or anti-memory in the ironic guise of a commitment to remembrance. The first approach is adopted, in very different ways and for very different reasons, by Marc Ellis and Amos Oz. The second approach is evident in the writing of Lawrence Langer and Moshe Zuckermann.

The focus of the discussion in this book has been on the variety of ways in which the Holocaust is perceived and remembered, and the controversy that this inevitably generates. Ellis and Oz both question whether it is possible to attach too much significance to remembrance of the Holocaust. Writing in 1987, Oz rhetorically asks: 'What is the weight of the past as opposed to the present and the future? Apart from the obligation to remember, is there also a right to forget?'[28] In his most recent book, Ellis speaks of 'ending Auschwitz'. Both suggest that the rhetoric surrounding the Holocaust can serve to desensitize its audience to subsequent instances of suffering, and even to justify the suffering of others. Writing of the Lebanon War, Oz points to certain, primarily political, uses of the Holocaust, the sub-text of which is that 'because they were victims in the past, the Jews are morally entitled to turn others into victims today.'[29] He is particularly critical of the then Prime Minister, Menachem Begin's use of Holocaust analogies to justify the Lebanon War and the bombing of civilian districts of Beirut.[30] Ellis broadens Oz's specific critique of political (mis)uses of the Holocaust into a more general attack on the centrality of these events in contemporary Jewish self-understanding. His central thesis is that Auschwitz (as *the* symbol of the Holocaust) has become 'a place where we can hide our accountability in the present, even as we demand it insistently of others for their past actions'.[31] Much of Ellis's work can be read as a sustained critique of the way in which the Holocaust has been mobilized to justify both the establishment of the State of Israel and the oppression of the Palestinian people. He argues that the mythologization of the Holocaust (with its emphasis upon the uniqueness of Jewish suffering) has proved damaging in the extreme and is now a 'burden' to the Jewish people: it has enabled Jews, particularly in Israel, to evade assuming moral responsibility for their actions towards the Palestinians.[32] For Ellis, therefore, 'to end Auschwitz is to admit that we are no longer innocent and that Israel is not our redemption.'[33] Needless to say, such an assertion strikes at the very roots of the myth of Holocaust and Redemption.

On the surface, Langer and Zuckermann read the situation very differently. Both suggest that rather than 'ending Auschwitz', there is a need to begin confronting the reality of what Auschwitz (and the Holocaust) represent. They agree with Ellis and Oz in questioning the value of some forms of Holocaust remembrance. However, both seem to suggest that before 'ending Auschwitz' it is necessary truly to confront it. Writing in 1988, Zuckerman suggests that the 'myth of Holocaust and Redemption' has enabled the majority of Israelis to avoid such a confrontation: 'From the beginning Israel repressed the Holocaust and used a *Holocaust-image* as a quasi concrete historical illustration for the right of the formation, existence and development of a Zionist state in all its phases – including the occupation after 1967.'[34] He suggests that the myth of the Holocaust, as narrated by Israeli civil religion, is a 'code' cultivated so that a surface memory of the Holocaust prevents the events penetrating 'too deeply into the collective consciousness'.[35] Public encounters with the memory of the Holocaust, such as the Eichmann trial or the official ceremonies on Yom Hashoah are 'stage-managed' representations of this 'image'.

Langer approaches the question from a different but complementary angle. He suggests that there are two approaches to remembering the Holocaust: a 'discourse of consolation' and a 'discourse of ruin'.[36] Using Langer's categories, the myth of Holocaust and Redemption falls into the category of a 'discourse of consolation'. By linking the Holocaust to the State of Israel, which is then interpreted in (implicitly or explicitly) redemptive terms, this myth presents a 'manageable version' of these events.[37] It allows for the possibility of consolation, a possibility that is absent in a 'discourse of ruin'. For Langer, such responses reflect a 'need to make the Holocaust more harmless than it was'.[38] By contrast, a 'discourse of ruin' stresses the absence of any redemptive meaning in the Holocaust. To confront and remember the Holocaust is to acknowledge this absence. Langer suggests that, to date, few have been willing to confront the Holocaust in such a way. As a consequence, while there is a well-established 'discourse of consolation', 'no full-fledged discourse of ruin, more appropriate to our hapless times, has yet emerged.'[39] Until there is such a confrontation, it is precipitate to speak of 'ending Auschwitz'.

The danger inherent in such a differentiation between a 'discourse of consolation' and a 'discourse of ruin' is that the implication is that one is more 'authentic' than the other. On what basis is such a judgement to be made? If one looks at the testimony of victims and survivors, it is possible to find evidence of both approaches. One of the characteristics of a mythological interpretation of the Holocaust is that while it allows for numerous contradictions and inconsistencies, it does nevertheless offer a cohesive framework suggesting a single message or meaning that is to be drawn from the memory of these events. An obvious criticism is that there are in fact a multiplicity of events and narratives within the rubric of 'the Holocaust'. As Langer himself repeatedly states, there are numerous 'versions' of these events, rather than one single, overarching narrative.[40] The variety of forms of remembrance reflect this multiplicity, as do the (sometimes competing or conflicting) narratives of Poles, Gypsies, Germans and so on. The myth of Holocaust and Redemption is one of these many 'versions'. The challenge today is to find ways of remembering/commemorating/teaching/studying the

Holocaust that acknowledge the existence of this plurality, while also allowing for the possibility that these various 'versions' of events might in fact have something to say to, and learn from, each other. The spate of controversies over memory and commemoration of the Holocaust suggests that there is a continuing quest for an 'authentic' way of representing these events. By reference to what criteria is such 'authenticity' to be judged? Are these criteria identical for all people, in all places, and at all times? Or do they vary, reflecting the experience of those involved?

The challenge is to find a way of speaking about the Holocaust that both acknowledges this plurality and is open to understanding each 'version' on its own terms, while also articulating a methodology that allows ethical judgements to be made about the contents or consequences of particular 'versions' of the Holocaust. To acknowledge the existence of a variety of 'versions' of the Holocaust is not to advocate a weak pluralism in which 'anything goes'. Rather, it is to argue that such plurality is the context in which any attempt to remember the Holocaust takes place. In effect, it is to understand discourse about the Holocaust as participation in an ongoing (critical) conversation, rather than as a series of monologues. Thus, as James Young suggests, perhaps one of the most enriching ways of remembering the Holocaust is currently to be found in the continuing debates over what and how we remember.[41]

NOTES

1. Moshe Zuckermann, 'The Curse of Forgetting: Israel and the Holocaust' (*Telos* Winter 1988/9, 78), pp. 43–54, p. 47.

2. Marc Ellis, *Beyond Innocence and Redemption* (New York: Harper & Row, 1990), p. 33.

3. Charles Maier, *The Unmasterable Past* (Cambridge: Harvard University Press, 1988), p. 165.

4. Charles Liebman, 'Myth, Tradition and Values in Israeli Society' (*Midstream* January 1978), pp. 44–53, p. 44.

5. Charles Liebman and Steven Cohen, *Two Worlds of Judaism* (New Haven: Yale University Press, 1990), p. 15.

6. Adi Ophir, 'On Sanctifying the Holocaust' (*Tikkun* 1987, 2:1), pp. 61–66, p. 63.

7. Claude Lanzmann, 'Shoah as Counter-Myth' (*Jewish Quarterly* Spring 1986), pp. 11–12, p. 12. For further discussion of the mythologization of the Holocaust, see Ophir, 'On Sanctifying the Holocaust', and Jonathan

Webber, 'Creating a New Inscription at Auschwitz-Birkenau: A Short Chapter in the Mythologization of the Holocaust' in Jon Davies and Isabel Wollaston (eds.), *The Sociology of Sacred Texts* (Sheffield Academic Press, 1993), pp. 45–58.

8. See: Jacob Neusner, *Stranger at Home* (Chicago: Chicago University Press, 1981); *The Jewish War against the Jews* (New York: KTAV, 1984); *Death and Birth of Judaism* (New York: Basic Books, 1987).

9. Neusner, *Death and Birth of Judaism*, p. 13.

10. Michael Berenbaum, *After Tragedy and Triumph* (CUP, 1990), p. 131.

11. Neusner, *Death and Birth of Judaism*, p. 279.

12. Such a 'messianic' interpretation of events is found in Eliezer Berkovits, *Faith after the Holocaust* (New York: KTAV, 1973), pp. 144–69. Elie Wiesel's treatment of the return to the Western Wall in *A Beggar in Jerusalem* (New York: Schocken Books, 1985) could also be interpreted in this light (pp. 190–202). However he warns against drawing any simplistic equation between the Holocaust and the State of Israel, and is careful to stress that 'victory does not prevent suffering from having existed, nor death from having taken its toll . . . of course the mystery of good is no less disturbing than the mystery of evil. But one does not cancel out the other' (p. 210). See also Wiesel's essays: 'Postwar: 1948' and 'Postwar: 1967' in *One Generation After* (New York: Schocken Books, 1982), pp. 126–37; and 'To a Brother in Israel' in *A Jew Today* (New York: Vintage Books, 1978), pp. 129–37.

13. Neusner, *Death and Birth of Judaism*, p. 195.

14. Charles Liebman and Eliezer Don-Yehiya, *Civil Religion in Israel* (Berkeley: University of California Press, 1983), p. 4. For further discussion of Israeli civil religion, see Myron Aronoff, 'Civil Religion in Israel' (*RAIN* 1981, 44), pp. 2–6; Lawrence Silberstein (ed.), *New Perspectives on Israeli History* (New York: New York University Press, 1991), pp. 155–224.

15. S. N. Herman, *Jewish Identity: A Social Psychological Perspective*, Second Edition (New Brunswick: Transaction Publishers, 1989), p. 43.

16. Irving Greenberg, *The Jewish Way: Living the Holidays* (New York: Summit Books, 1988), p. 363.

17. For more detail on the role of the Holocaust/Yom Hashoah and Yom Haatzmaut in Israel, see: Amos Elon, *The Israelis: Founders and Sons* (Penguin, 1983), pp. 198–221; Don Handelmann, *Models and Mirrors: Towards an Anthropology of Public Events* (CUP, 1990), pp. 191–223; James E. Young, *The Texture of Memory* (New Haven: Yale University Press, 1993), pp. 263–81.

18. Simon Rawidowicz, *Studies in Jewish Thought* (Philadelphia: JPSA, 1974), p. 221.

19. Moshe Dayan, cited in Tom Segev, *The Seventh Million* (New York: Hill & Wang, 1993), p. 369.

20. Lt. Gen. Ehud Barak, Auschwitz, April 1993, in *Jerusalem Post International Edition* (week ending 18.4.92), p. 28.

21. Neusner, *Death and Birth of Judaism*, p. 280.

22. Neusner, *Death and Birth of Judaism*, p. 282.

23. Jacob Neusner, 'Memorials of Mistrust' (*Jewish Chronicle* 23.4.93).

24. Jonathan Sacks, *Crisis and Covenant* (Manchester University Press, 1993), p. 102.

25. Jacob Neusner, 'The Implications of the Holocaust' (*Journal of Religion* 1973, 53:3), pp. 293–308, p. 308.

26. Jonathan Woocher, *Sacred Survival* (Bloomington: Indiana University Press, 1986), p. 131.

27. See Michael Berenbaum, *After Tragedy and Triumph*, pp. 3–16; Elli Wohlgelernter, 'Museums Carry the Past into the Future' (*Jerusalem Post International Edition*, week ending 24.4.93), pp. 16A–16B.

28. Amos Oz, *The Slopes of Lebanon* (Vintage Books, 1991), p. 123.

29. Oz, *The Slopes of Lebanon*, p. 58.

30. 'Hitler's Dead, Mr. Prime Minister' in *The Slopes of Lebanon*. See also: Rochelle Saidel, 'The Holocaust in the Political Culture of Israel' (*Midstream* 1989, 35:7), pp. 17–21; Tom Segev, *The Seventh Million*, pp. 396–404.

31. Marc Ellis, *Ending Auschwitz* (Louisville: Westminster John Knox Press, 1994), p. 24.

32. Ellis, *Ending Auschwitz*, p. 40.

33. Ellis, *Ending Auschwitz*, p. 41.

34. Zuckermann, 'The Curse of Forgetting', p. 45.

35. Zuckermann, 'The Curse of Forgetting', p. 47.

36. Lawrence Langer, *Admitting the Holocaust* (OUP, 1995), p. 7.

37. Langer, *Admitting the Holocaust*, p. 9.

38. Langer, *Admitting the Holocaust*, p. 184.

39. Langer, *Admitting the Holocaust*, p. 7.

40. Lawrence Langer, *Versions of Survival* (Albany: State University of New York Press, 1982).

41. Young, *The Texture of Memory*, pp. xi, 81.

BIBLIOGRAPHY

Abrahamson, I., ed., *Against Silence: The Voice and Vision of Elie Wiesel*. 3 vols. New York, Holocaust Library, 1985.

Adelson, A. and Lapides, R., eds., *Lodz Ghetto: Inside a Community Under Siege*. New York, Viking, 1989.

Alter, R., 'Deformations of the Holocaust' (*Commentary* February 1981), pp. 48–54.

Améry, J., *At the Mind's Limits: Contemplations by a Survivor on Auschwitz and its Realities*. New York, Schocken Books, 1986.

Arendt, H., *Eichmann in Jerusalem: A Report on the Banality of Evil*. Revised and Enlarged Edition. Penguin 1965.

Aronoff, M., 'Civil Religion in Israel' (*RAIN* 1981, 44), pp. 2–6.

Ascherson, N., 'The Shoah Controversy' (*Soviet-Jewish Affairs* 1986, 16:1), pp. 53–61.

—— 'Remains of the Abomination' (*Independent on Sunday Review* 22.1.95), pp. 12–16.

Avisar, I., *Screening the Holocaust: Cinema's Images of the Unimaginable*. Bloomington, Indiana University Press, 1988.

Bartoszewski, W. T., *The Convent at Auschwitz*. Bowerdean Press 1990.

Bauer, Y., *The Holocaust in Historical Perspective*. Sheldon Press 1978.

Bauman, Z., *Modernity and the Holocaust*. Polity Press 1991.

Belitsky, H. M., 'Memory and Accidental Tourists' (*Hadassah Magazine* 1993, 74:8), pp. 26–9.

Berenbaum, M., *After Tragedy and Triumph: Modern Jewish Thought and the American Experience*. CUP 1990.

—— *The World Must Know: The History of the Holocaust as Told in the United States Holocaust Memorial Museum*. Boston, Little, Brown & Company, 1993.

Berger, J., 'The Peril of Vulgarization' (*Dimensions* 1989, 5:1), pp. 3–6.

Berkovits, E., *Faith after the Holocaust*. New York, KTAV, 1973.

Bernstein, M. A., *Foregone Conclusions: Against Apocalyptic History*. Berkeley, University of California Press, 1994.

Bettelheim, B., *On Surviving and Other Essays*. Thames & Hudson 1979.

Blair, J., 'Spielberg Comes of Age' (*Esquire* March 1994), pp. 62–6.

Blanchot, M., *Writing the Disaster*. Lincoln, University of Nebraska Press, 1986.

Bryk, A., 'Poland and the Memory of the Holocaust' (*Partisan Review* 1990, 57:2), pp. 228–38.

Buruma, I., 'The Misleading Mystique of Mass Extermination' (*Spectator* 28.1.95), pp. 9–11.

Cesarani, D., ed., *The Final Solution*. Routledge 1994.

Dafni, R., ed., *Yad Vashem*. Fifth Edition. Jerusalem, Yad Vashem, 1990.

Davies, J. and Wollaston, I., eds., *The Sociology of Sacred Texts*. Sheffield Academic Press 1993.

De Saint-Cheron, P. and Wiesel, E., *Evil and Exile*. Notre Dame, University of Notre Dame Press, 1990.

Doneson, J., *The Holocaust and American Film*. Philadelphia, JPSA, 1987.

Ellis, M., *Beyond Innocence and Redemption: Creating a Moral Future for the Jewish People*. San Francisco, Harper & Row, 1990.

—— *Ending Auschwitz: The Future of Jewish and Christian Life*. Louisville, Westminster John Knox Press, 1994.

Elon, A., *The Israelis: Founders and Sons*. Penguin 1983.

Evron, B., 'The Holocaust: Learning the Wrong Lessons' (*Journal of Palestinian Studies* 1981, 10), pp. 16–26.

Ezrahi, S. D., *By Words Alone: The Holocaust in Literature*. Chicago, University of Chicago Press, 1980.

Fackenheim, E. L., *God's Presence in History*. New York, Schocken Books, 1970.

—— *The Jewish Return into History: Reflections in the Age of Auschwitz and a New Jerusalem*. New York, Schocken Books, 1978.

—— *To Mend the World: Foundations of Future Jewish Thought*. New York, Schocken Books, 1982.

—— 'Jewish Values in a Post-Holocaust Future' (*Judaism* 1967, 16:3), pp. 266–99.

—— 'The Development of My Thought' (*Religious Studies Review* 1987, 13:3), pp. 204–6.

Felman, S. and Laub, D., *Testimony: Crises of Witnessing in Literature, Psychoanalysis, and History*. Routledge 1992.

Fleischner, E., ed., *Auschwitz: Beginning of a New Era?* New York, KTAV, 1977.

Friedlander, S., ed., *Probing the Limits of Representation*. Cambridge, Harvard University Press, 1992.

Garber, Z. and Zuckerman, B., 'Why Do We Call the Holocaust "the Holocaust"?' (*Modern Judaism* May 1989), pp. 197–211.

Gill, B., 'The Holocaust Museum: An Unquiet Sanctuary' (*New Yorker* 19.4.93), pp. 107-9.

Greenberg, G., 'Orthodox Theological Responses to *Kristallnacht*' (*Holocaust and Genocide Studies* 1988, 3:4), pp. 431–42.

Greenberg, I. and Rosenfeld, A., eds., *Confronting the Holocaust: The Impact of Elie Wiesel*. Bloomington, Indiana University Press, 1978.

Handelmann, D., *Models and Mirrors: Towards an Anthropology of Public Events*. CUP 1990.

Hartman, G., ed., *Bitburg in Moral and Political Perspective*. Bloomington, Indiana University Press, 1986.

—— ed., *Holocaust Remembrance: The Shapes of Memory*. Basil Blackwell 1994.

Hayes, P., ed., *Lessons and Legacies: The Meaning of the Holocaust in a Changing World*. Evanston, Northwestern University Press, 1991.

Heller, Z., 'The Real Thing' (*Independent on Sunday Review* 23.5.93), pp. 24–8.

Herman, S. N., *Jewish Identity: A Social Psychological Perspective*. Second Edition. New Brunswick, Transaction Publishers, 1989.

Insdorf, A., *Indelible Shadows: Film and the Holocaust*. Second Edition. CUP 1989.

Irwin-Zarecka, I., *Neutralizing Memory: The Jew in Contemporary Poland*. New Brunswick, Transaction Publishers, 1989.

Jacobs, S., *Rethinking Jewish Faith: The Child of a Survivor Responds*. Albany, State University of New York Press, 1994.

Jakobovits, I., 'Some Personal, Theological and Religious Reflections on the Holocaust' (*Holocaust and Genocide Studies* 1988, 3:4), pp. 371–81.

Jick, L. 'The Holocaust: Its Use and Abuse within the American Public' (*Yad Vashem Studies* 1981, 14), pp. 303–15.

Kaplan, C., *Scroll of Agony: A Diary of the Warsaw Ghetto*. Hamish Hamilton 1966.

Katz, S., *Post-Holocaust Dialogues*. New York, New York University Press, 1983.

—— *The Holocaust in Historical Context*. Vol. 1. OUP 1994.

Kermish, J., ed., *To Live with Honor and Die with Honor! Selected Documents from the Warsaw Ghetto Underground Archives 'O.S.' ['Oneg Shabbath']*. Jerusalem, Yad Vashem, 1986.

Kirschner, R., *Rabbinic Responses of the Holocaust Era*. New York, Schocken Books, 1985.

Kren, G. and Rappoport, L., *The Holocaust and the Crisis of Human Behaviour*. Revised Edition. New York, Holmes & Meier, 1994.

Kritzmann, L., ed., *Auschwitz and After: Race, Culture, and 'The Jewish Question' in France*. Routledge 1995.

Kushner, T., *The Holocaust and the Liberal Imagination*. Basil Blackwell 1994.

Lang, B., ed., *Writing and the Holocaust*. New York, Holmes & Meier, 1988.

Langer, L., *Versions of Survival: The Holocaust and the Human Spirit*. Albany, State University of New York Press, 1982.

—— *Holocaust Testimonies: The Ruins of Memory*. New Haven, Yale University Press, 1991.

—— *Admitting the Holocaust: Collected Essays*. OUP 1995.

—— 'Tainted Memory: Remembering the Warsaw Ghetto' (*Tikkun* 1993, 8:3), pp. 37–40, 85–90.

Lanzmann, C., *Shoah: An Oral History of the Holocaust*. New York, Pantheon, 1985.

—— 'From the Holocaust to "*Holocaust*" ' (*Dissent* 1981, 28:2), pp. 188–94.

—— '*Shoah* as Counter-Myth' (*Jewish Quarterly* Spring 1986), pp. 11–12.

—— 'The Twisted Truth of *Schindler's List*' (*Evening Standard* 10.2.94).

Lerman, A., 'The Art of Holocaust Remembering' (*Jewish Quarterly* 1989, 135), pp. 24–32.

Lerner, M., 'Victims and Victimizers' (*Tikkun* 1994, 9:2), pp. 7–9.

Levi, P., *If This Is a Man / The Truce*. Abacus 1987.

—— *Moments of Reprieve*. Abacus 1987.

—— *The Drowned and the Saved*. Michael Joseph 1988.

—— *Collected Poems*. Faber & Faber 1992.

Levkov, I., ed., *Bitburg and Beyond*. New York, Shapolsky Books, 1987.

Liebman, C. and Don-Yehiya, E., *Civil Religion in Israel: Traditional Judaism and Political Culture in the Jewish State*. Berkeley, University of California Press, 1983.

Liebman, C. and Cohen, S., *Two Worlds of Judaism*. New Haven, Yale University Press, 1990.

Liebman, C. 'Myth, Tradition and Values in Israeli Society' (*Midstream* January 1978), pp. 44–53.

Lipstadt, D., 'Invoking the Holocaust' (*Judaism* 1981, 30:3), pp. 335–43.

Lopate, P., 'Resistance to the Holocaust' (*Tikkun* 1989, 4:3), pp. 55–65.

Louvish, S., 'Witness' (*Sight and Sound* 1994, 4:3), pp. 12–15.

Lustigman, M., *Kindness and the Art of Reading Ashes*. New York, Peter Lang, 1988.

Lyotard, J. F., *The Differend*. Manchester University Press 1988.

—— *Heidegger and 'the jews'*. Minneapolis, University of Minneapolis Press, 1990.

Maier, C., *The Unmasterable Past: History, Holocaust and German National Identity*. Cambridge, Harvard University Press, 1988.

Marrus, M., *The Holocaust in History*. Weidenfeld & Nicolson 1988.

—— ed., *The Nazi Holocaust*. 15 vols. Westport, Meckler, 1989.

Miles, J., 'Auschwitz and Sarajevo' (*Tikkun* 1994, 9:2), pp. 17–20, 91–2.

Miller, J., *One, by One, by One: Facing the Holocaust*. Weidenfeld & Nicolson 1990.

Milton, S., *In Fitting Memory: The Art and Politics of Holocaust Memorials*. Detroit, Wayne State University Press, 1991.

Mintz, A., *Hurban*. New York, Columbia University Press, 1984.

Neusner, J., *Stranger at Home: 'The Holocaust', Zionism and American Judaism*. Chicago, Chicago University Press, 1981.

—— *The Jewish War against the Jews: Reflections on Golah, Shoah and Torah*. New York, KTAV, 1984.

—— *Death and Birth of Judaism: The Impact of Christianity, Secularism, and the Holocaust on Jewish Faith*. New York, Basic Books, 1987.

—— 'Implications of the Holocaust' (*Journal of Religion* 1973, 53:3), pp. 293–308.

Ophir, A., 'On Sanctifying the Holocaust: An Anti-Theological Treatise' (*Tikkun* 1987, 2:1), pp. 61–6.

Ophuls, M., 'Closely Watched Trains' (*American Film* November 1985), pp. 16–27, 79.

Oz, A., *The Slopes of Lebanon*. Vintage 1991.

Pacy, J. and Wertheimer, A. P., eds., *Perspectives on the Holocaust: Essays in Honor of Raul Hilberg*. Boulder, Westview Press, 1995.

Polonsky, A., ed., *My Brother's Keeper? Recent Polish Debates on the Holocaust*. Routledge 1990.

Rabinbach, A. and Zipes, J., eds., *Germans and Jews after the Holocaust*. New York, Holmes & Meier, 1986.

Rafferty, T., 'A Man of Transactions' (*New Yorker* 20.12.93), pp. 129–32.

Ringelblum, E., *Notes from the Warsaw Ghetto*. New York, Schocken Books, 1974.

Rittner, C. and Roth, J., eds., *Memory Offended: The Auschwitz Convent Controversy*. New York, Praeger, 1991.

Rosenbaum, I., *Holocaust and Halakhah*. New York, KTAV, 1976.

Rosenberg, A. and Myers, G., eds., *Echoes from the Holocaust: Philosophical Reflections on a Dark Theme*. Philadelphia, Temple University Press, 1988.

Rosenberg, B. and Heuman, F., eds., *Theological and Halakhic Reflections on the Holocaust*. New York, KTAV, 1992.

Rosenfeld, A., *A Double Dying: Reflections on Holocaust Literature*. Bloomington, Indiana University Press, 1980.

Roskies, D., *Against the Apocalypse*. Cambridge, Harvard University Press, 1984.

—— ed., *The Literature of Destruction*. Philadelphia, JPSA, 1989.

Rubenstein, R., *The Cunning of History: Mass Death and the American Future*. New York, Harper & Row, 1975.

—— *After Auschwitz*. Second Edition. Baltimore, John Hopkins University Press, 1992.

Ryback, T., 'Evidence of Evil' (*New Yorker* 15.11.93), pp. 68–81.

Sacks, J. *Tradition in an Untraditional Age*. Vallentine Mitchell 1990.

—— *Crisis and Covenant: Jewish Thought after the Holocaust*. Manchester University Press 1993.

—— *Faith in the Future*. Darton, Longman & Todd 1995.

Saidel, R., 'The Role of the Holocaust in the Political Culture of Israel' (*Midstream* 1989, 35:7), pp. 17–21.

Segev, T., *The Seventh Million: The Israelis and the Holocaust*. New York, Hill & Wang, 1993.

Silberstein, L., ed., *New Perspectives on Israeli History*. New York, New York University Press, 1991.

Styron, W., *Sophie's Choice*. Corgi 1980.

Świebocki, T. & H., eds., *Auschwitz: Voices from the Ground*. Oświęcim, Państowe Muzeum Oświęcim-Brzezinka, 1992.

Tal, U., 'On the Study of Holocaust and Genocide' (*Yad Vashem Studies* 1979, 13), pp. 7–52.

Telpaz, G., 'An Interview with William Styron' (*Partisan Review* 1985, 52:3), pp. 252–63.

Wapshott, N., 'Return of the Prodigal' (*The Times Magazine* 15.1.94), pp. 7–9.

Webber, J., *The Future of Auschwitz: Some Personal Reflections*. The First Frank Green Lecture. Oxford Centre for Postgraduate Hebrew Studies 1992.

—— ed., *Jewish Identities in the New Europe*. Littman Library of Jewish Civilization 1994.

Webber, J. and Wilsack, C., eds., *Auschwitz: A History in Photographs*. Bloomington, Indiana University Press, 1993.

Wiesel, E., *Messengers of God*. New York, Summit Books, 1976.

—— *A Jew Today*. New York, Vintage Books, 1979.

—— *Legends of Our Times*. New York, Schocken Books, 1982.

—— *One Generation After*. New York, Schocken Books, 1982.

—— *From the Kingdom of Memory*. New York, Summit Books, 1990.

—— *Sages and Dreamers*. New York, Touchstone, 1991.

—— 'A Personal Response' (*Face to Face* 1979, 6), pp. 35–7.

Wieseltier, L., 'After Memory' (*New Republic* 2.5.93), pp. 14–26.

Woocher, J., *Sacred Survival: The Civil Religion of American Jews*. Bloomington, Indiana University Press, 1986.

Wohlgelernter, E., 'Museums Carry the Past into the Future' (*Jerusalem Post International Edition*, week ending 24.4.93), pp. 16A–16B.

Wolffsohn, M., *Eternal Guilt? Forty Years of German-Jewish Relations*. New York, Columbia University Press, 1993.

Yerushalmi, Y. H., *Zakhor*. New York, Schocken Books, 1982.

Young, J. E., *Writing and Rewriting the Holocaust: Narrative and the Consequences of Interpretation*. Bloomington, Indiana University Press, 1988.

—— *The Texture of Memory: Holocaust Memorials and Meaning*. New Haven, Yale University Press, 1993.

—— ed., *The Art of Memory: Holocaust Memorials in History*. Munich, Prestel-Verlag, 1994.

—— 'The Future of Auschwitz' (*Tikkun* 1992, 7:6), pp. 31–3, 77.

—— 'The Veneration of Ruins' (*Yale Journal of Criticism* 1993, 6:2), pp. 275–83.

Zuckermann, M., 'The Curse of Forgetting: Israel and the Holocaust' (*Telos* 1988–9, 78), pp. 43–54.

INDEX

101